A CELTIC CHRISTOLOGY

A Celtic Christology

The Incarnation according to John Scottus Eriugena

John F. Gavin, S.J.

WITH A FOREWORD BY
John Panteleimon Manoussakis

CASCADE *Books* · Eugene, Oregon

A CELTIC CHRISTOLOGY
The Incarnation according to John Scottus Eriugena

Cascade Books
An Imprint of Wipf and Stock Publishers
199 W. 8th Ave., Suite 3
Eugene, OR 97401

www.wipfandstock.com

ISBN 13: 978-1-62564-464-0

Cataloguing-in-Publication data:

Gavin, John, 1968–.

    A Celtic Christology : the Incarnation according to John Scottus Eriugena / John Gavin, S.J. ; with a foreword by John Panteleimon Manoussakis.

    xviii + 160 pp. ; 23 cm. Includes bibliographical references and indexes.

    ISBN 13: 978-1-62564-464-0

    1. Erigena, Johannes Scotus, approximately 810–approximately 877. 2. Incarnation. 3. Incarnation—History of doctrines. I. Manoussakis, John Panteleimon. II. Title.

B765.J34 G38 2014

Manufactured in the U.S.A.

To my brothers and sisters:
Ellen, Tom, Tim, Dan, Brendan, Mary, and Patrick.
For their love and support on the journey.

And to my Jesuit brothers. AMDG.

"In my Father's house there are many rooms; if it were not so, would I have told you that I go to prepare a place for you? And when I go and prepare a place for you, I will come again and will take you to myself, that where I am you may be also."

JOHN 14:2–3

Quae mens, quae virtus, superum quae facta sophia
in carnem poterit descensum dicere verbi,
carnis et in verbum sublimia bimata nosse?

—IOHANNES SCOTTUS ERIUGENA, *CARMINA* XXV

Contents

Foreword

John Scottus Eriugena lived in a world that was still characterized by the desire to dwell in mysteries, not by the aptitude for solving perplexities. His theological style will disappoint anyone looking to be impressed by the grandeur of the struggle, of the continuous effort, to uphold and reconcile incompatible systems of thought. The intelligibility of being is yet to be fragmented and thought is still preserved and presented in a unified vision. What one meets in Eriugena's work is the confidence in God's self-revelation through complementing the manifestations of his creation and his Incarnation—a revelation not awaiting to be discovered, but to be *seen* and to be *lived*. The calmness of his work reflects this confidence that finds its correspondence in a vision that remains integrated and whole.

Themes that for some time now have been treated as distinct topics—Christology, anthropology, metaphysics, eschatology, and so on—are difficult, if not impossible, to be separated from each other in Eriugena's thought. And it would be a mistake to single out any of these, treating them in isolation from the whole to which they belong. These aspects of Eriugena's theological system are like musical themes, leitmotivs even. Yet, unlike our contemporary understanding of music, Eriugena's compositions are not like the sonatas or the symphonies of the Classical and Romantic eras, for which the musical theme is a singular and unique moment, a musical phrase or idea that can stand on its own as an event and as the eventful, connected by other isolated themes only through the familial resemblances of harmonic modulation. Rather, Eriugena's theology is more like the linear complexity of Johann Sebastian Bach's chorales. The theme, if one could still speak of a theme, permeates the whole and it reverberates and echoes throughout the entire composition. Like Johann Sebastian

Bach, who brought together in his music the distinct styles of North and South Europe, so Eriugena combines the Augustinian West with the Dionysian East—a valuable example and resource for our ecumenical efforts.

To put it differently, our reading of Eriugena, as with many of his contemporaries, has been subjected to the distortion of knowledge's progressive fragmentation that can be traced, if only in quick outline, by looking at the ways that each period aspired to present its self-understanding to itself, while passing it down to future generations: for the Medievals this presentation took the form of the *summa*; for the Moderns it was the *encyclopedia*; one could say that today we have moved beyond modernity to a new period marked by the advent of *Wikipedia*. On the one hand, for the *summae* knowledge was understood in its all-encompassing nature, where each article presupposes the previous one and anticipates the following in an interlocking fashion that is, at once, systematic and synthetic, so that it merits the often-invoked comparison to the architecture of the Gothic cathedrals. The encyclopedias of the Enlightenment, on the other hand, are organized by the arbitrariness of the alphabet, so that one entry follows the next without so much of a presumption to any connection or logical necessity other than the accidental fact of sharing the same initial letter. The encyclopedic arrangement is only symptomatic of the arbitrariness and accidental character that had infected knowledge itself well before its codification in dictionaries and encyclopedias. On the way from the *summa* to the encyclopedia, the whole was lost.

How are we to recapture it? The greatest strength of Fr. Gavin's book lies precisely in this: in representing an effort to restore the continuity of experience in Eriugena's thought. The proto-scholastic arrangement of the *Periphyseon* is read in light of his liturgical hymnology, while Eriugena the philosopher is not separated from Eriugena the homilist and commentator. Fr. Gavin seeks—and in the humble opinion of this reader succeeds—in rehabilitating Eriugena's theology within its ecclesial, liturgical, and sacramental context—a context that, as he shows, makes little sense in the absence of a robust Christology.[1] For too long and for too many scholars, Eriugena has been read as little more than a Christianized Neoplatonist.

The accusation is, of course, quite familiar. It was brought with the same force against Eriugena's Eastern mentor, Dionysius the pseudo-Aeropagite;

---

1. The author's criticism of the Irishman's failure to incorporate successfully the Maximian theology of the two wills might be indicative of an incomplete appropriation on Eriugena's part of Chalcedonean Christology.

but it has today collapsed, thanks to the efforts of more recent and more attentive readings of his corpus.[2] The present work aspires to render the same service to Dionysius' student. This is not to deny, of course, the all-too-evident influence of Neoplatonism (as it should be expected, since what other philosophical language did the Christian thinkers of the time have at their disposal that could become a suitable instrument, an *organon*, for constructing their theologies?), which becomes for his poetic mind, as poetic as any Irishman's, the inspiration for some daring conclusions that would justly sound strange to orthodox ears. Yet, at the end of the day, Eriugena's allegiances are unambiguous for, in Fr. Gavin's reading, he emerges not as a Christianized Neoplatonist, but merely as a Neoplatonic Christian. One may think that the difference here is only one of emphasis; nevertheless, it is an emphasis that makes all the difference.

The most decisive aspect of the reversal between these two epithets is the centrality that the concept of creation occupies in Eriugena's work. Indeed, his fourfold division is organized around the sole criterion of creation; that is, the whole is divided into a) that which creates but is not created; b) that which creates and is created; c) that which is created but does not create; and d) that which neither creates nor is created. What distinguishes, therefore, the four realms of being is, what we may call after Heidegger, not an ontological difference, but rather a *ktisiological* difference—that is, the difference between created and uncreated orders.

Here a word of clarification of the terminology is in order. As the foregoing remarks should have made immediately clear, and in spite of Eriugena's own employment of the term *natura*, and against the very title of his magnum opus (*Peri-physeon*), what determines his thought, and what ultimately separates him from a Porphyry or even an Eckhart, is not *natura*, but *creatura*—the passing from *physis* to *ktisis*.

The difference between these two terms that have come to be used today largely as synonyms is a telling one. As any student of ancient philosophy would know, nature is simply what keeps flowing out of a primordial source. Nature is also that primordial source itself that remains "hidden."[3] In this conception, nature stands in opposition to creation—see, for example, the binary polarity between φύσει and τέχνῃ that organizes

---

2. For a summary of the conflicting interpretations of Dionsysius and a new approach see Perl, *Theophany*, 2.

3. On Heraclitus' famous fragment φύσις κρύπτεσθαι φιλεῖ (Diels-Kranz, fr. 123) see Pierre Hadot's magisterial analysis in *The Veil of Isis: An Essay on the History of the Idea of Nature*.

Aristotelian metaphysics—for nature is itself its own origin, or rather the lack of an origin (*Abgrund*). Several classical ideas find their birthplace in this image of the aboriginal flowing of nature (*physis*): nature's anarchy and thus eternity; nature's emanation; nature's divinity.[4] In all these concepts the prevailing thought is that of nature's *necessity*. For classical thought, *physis* exists *necessarily*. Its necessary character scorns man's contingency.

On the other hand, the scriptural idea of creation underscores the world's *contingency*, for there was a time that the world did not exist, nor had to exist. Furthermore, the creation of the world "in the beginning" (Gen 1:1) dispels any illusions of eternity and allows for the mystery of time and history to be positively evaluated. And because, unlike nature, creation is neither eternal nor divine, it can now be known (hence the inception of modern science). Above all, however, the concept of creation encompasses humanity and the world together and not in some opposition. Thus the metaphysics of the *ktisiological* difference has some decisive anthropological implications.

In the Christian tradition, the world is always thought not apart from humanity, but together with it, as man is never thought apart from the world. So, for St. Maximus the Confessor, for example, man cannot be saved apart from the world; that is, the world is the ladder that man needs to employ in order to reach his salvation, a ladder that, unlike Wittgenstein's, he never kicks off once he has reached his destination—especially since this same ladder was assumed by God in his Incarnation in order to reach man.[5] So the world, we could say, cannot be "saved" apart from man. Indeed, for the church fathers—and Eriugena follows in this line of tradition—the purpose of the world was man and this is why man is the *macrocosm* of the cosmos. Today we think precisely on opposite terms, so much so that it is difficult for us to understand how it is possible for man to be "larger," so to speak, than the universe. For us today the universe is larger than man (it is interesting here to take note of modernity's tendency to think of the world in spatial categories) and therefore, if an analogy is to be established

---

4. Aristotle preserves in his *De Anima* the apophthegmatic articulation of nature's divinity in a dictum attributed to Thales: πάντα πλήρη θεῶν εἶναι (A, 5, 411a7).

5. For the far-reaching (one could say without exaggeration "cosmic") implications of the Incarnation in Eriugena's work, see the second chapter of this book. Yet, it is precisely for these reasons that expressions from the first chapter of this book, such as "the inauthenticity of material expression" or "the inauthenticity of carnal expression", if left unqualified, make me feel rather uneasy (not to mention that the author's insights into what he calls an "environmental Christology" would otherwise be lost).

between the two, then we can understand man only as the *microcosm* of the universe. But if for a moment we stop thinking in spatial terms, then man encompasses the whole world, for man, in contemplating the world, not only recognizes its order (therefore its cosmic and "cosmetic" beauty) but also provides, or rather bestows in his priestly function, this order upon the world. This idea, traced through Gregory of Nyssa (in his *De opificio hominis*) to Dionysius the Aeropagite, to Maximus the Confessor, is finally received by Eriugena who boldly affirms that:

> In man every creature, both visible and invisible, is created. There-fore, he is said to be the "workshop of all things," since in him all things which come after God are contained. Thus he is customarily called an intermediary. Indeed, since he consists of body and soul, he contains within himself and gathers into unity the extremes that are at a distance from himself—that is, the spiritual and material.[6]

Since creation in general (that is, both the world and humanity) was not necessary, nor determined by any hidden necessity for God, but came about as an act of his freedom, the world and humanity are also partici-pants in that gift. That means that creation, and man along with it, are free to become themselves. "The manner in which *what* something is (given/ gift, being/eternal-being) emerges from *how* something is (well-being/non-being)."[7] What we have here is a revolutionary idea that breaks with the essentialism of classical philosophy, and particularly of Neoplatonism, and anticipates by some ten centuries existentialism's primacy to existence (the how) over essence (the what). It can indeed be expected as a matter of course that wherever the *ex nihilo* of creation is not properly thematized, then an essentialist metaphysics is in order. Eriugena, in situating his thought vis-à-vis creation, thinks consistently of the origin, of the beginning, that is of the *nothing*—to which, ironically, a theologian is not supposed to have recourse.[8] Yet, Eriugena's thought is made possible by a constant encounter with this very question: "why there is something rather than nothing?"

6. *Peri.* V, 49, 1517–23, the author's translation. Fr. Gavin dedicates a good part of this book's first chapter precisely to the topic of "Man's role in God's creation" implied here.

7. P. 93 below (emphasis in the original), and again later on: "[w]hile all return to God, this union does not stifle the distinct forms of participation: *who* one is and *how* one is as an individual shapes one's final state of participation in the divine." (p. 137, emphasis in the original).

8. At least according to Heidegger, who, in his polemical remarks against Christian-ity, assumes that a Christian, on account of his or her belief in a creator God, is unable to think the primordial nothing. Thus a "Christian philosophy is foolishness and a squared

The primacy of existence and existents—be they he who exists super-abundantly as the principle of existence or those who exist (literally, *ek-sist*) as derivative beings—avoids and indeed transforms the anonymity of being (what Levinas has called the *il y a*). Existence is made personal. This has an epistemological consequence: essence (the *what*, *quid est*, quiddity) can be known only through an existent (the *tropos* of hypostatic being). Here the ground is prepared for the famous Kierkegaardian principle of the Incarnation that reverses the classical hierarchy of ranking the universal higher than the particular and affords to the particular an infinite value—indeed the value of infinity. For the author of this work, this consequence has concrete ethical and theological ramifications, which the reader will undoubtedly find both enlightening and beneficial to discover in the pages that follow.

John Panteleimon Manoussakis
The Feast of St. Andrew, 2013

---

circle" (*Introduction to Metaphysics*).

Acknowledgements

DURING MY ORAL LICENSE EXAMINATION at the Augustinianum in Rome in 2004, I rashly stated that Eriugena's Christology was excessively platonic and lacked a sense of historicity. Prof. Giulio d'Onofrio rightfully challenged my words, encouraging me to examine the sources more broadly. His well-founded critique and guidance over the years have inspired me in writing this volume.

I am very grateful to the many individuals who helped me during the composition of this work. In particular, I would like to thank Fr. William Reiser, S.J., Fr. Michael McDermott, S.J., Fr. Paul Mankowski, S.J., and Fr. John Manoussakis for their careful reading of the manuscript in its various stages and for their invaluable advice in improving its quality. My editor, Dr. Robin Parry, my typesetter, Patrick Harrison, and the staff at Wipf and Stock have been generous and invaluable guides in the preparation of this volume. I am also grateful to Patrick Gavin for his proofreading of the text. Any remaining errors are my own.

I would like to thank the College of the Holy Cross for granting me the junior leave during the 2013–14 academic year that allowed me to complete this and other projects. My colleagues in the Department of Religious Studies continue to inspire me to seek the *magis* through their scholarship, dedication to teaching, and *cura personalis*. My students at Holy Cross made the hours of reading, writing, and reflection worthwhile.

The Jesuit community of Holy Cross, under the able guidance of the rector, Fr. John Savard, S.J., supported me in countless ways during the writing of this book. I am blessed to live among them.

Finally, I would like to thank my parents, John and Patricia Gavin, without whom this book would certainly never have seen the light.

A Note on Translations and Editions

Unless otherwise stated in the footnote, all translations are my own. This includes the *Carmina*. Though Michael Herren provides a superb translation in his edition, I have elected to prepare my renderings for the illustration of key points.

All citations from the *Periphyseon* are from CCM 161–65.

Abbreviations

Works of Johannes Scottus Eriugena

Carm.   *Carmina*

Comm.   *Commentarius in Sanctum Evangelium secundum Johannem*

Expo.   *Expositiones in Ierarchiam Coelestem*

Hom.   *Homilia in prologum Sancti Evangelii secundum Johannem*

Peri.   *Periphyseon (On the Division of Nature)*

Prae.   *De divina praedestinatione liber*

Series

CCG   *Corpus Christianorum Series Greca.* Turnhout: Brepols.

CCL   *Corpus Christianorum Series Latina.* Turnhout: Brepols.

CCM   *Corpus Christianorum Continuatio Medievalis.* Turnhout: Brepols.

CSEL   *Corpus Scriptorum Ecclesiasticorum Latinorum.* Vienna: Universität Salzburg.

GNO   *Gregorii Nysseni Opera.* Leiden: Brill.

LCL   *Loeb Classical Library.* Cambridge: Harvard University Press.

PG   *Patrologia Graeca.* Edited by J. P. Migne. Paris, 1857–66.

Abbreviations

PL	*Patrologia Latina*. Edited by J. P. Migne. Paris, 1844–64.
PTS	*Patristiche Texte und Studien*. Berlin: de Gruyter.
SC	*Sources Chretiennes*. Paris: Les Éditions du Cerf.
SLH	*Scriptores Latini Hiberniae*. Dublin: Dublin Institute for Advanced Studies.
SPES	Papers of the Society for the Promotion of Eriugenian Studies.

Introduction

In 1988, Ireland issued a five-pound note depicting a balding man with bushy eyebrows and a stern gaze. He stands huddled in a fur—apparently the garb of a Dark Ages intellectual—with a page from a Latin manuscript as the background. A single word identifies him: *Scotus*, Irishman. Unfortunately this monetary tribute has been eclipsed by the Euro and its subject has, in turn, fallen out of currency. Though certainly a name to his countrymen and to historians of Western thought, the scope of John Scottus Eriugena's genius remains little known.

Life

His origins remain veiled in shadow. His names indicate his native land— *Scottus* and *Eriugena* both mean "Irishman" in Latin and Greek—but it is impossible to offer anything more precise.[1] Even suggestions for his date of birth vary: scholars tend to estimate sometime between 800–815.[2] As for his status within the church, it is uncertain whether he was monk, priest, or one of the lay scholars who gave life to the remarkable intellectual flourishing of the age.[3]

There is no doubt, however, that Eriugena received an excellent intellectual and spiritual formation, both in his native Ireland and on the continent. This included a profound reading of the Scriptures and foundational texts in Latin, including: the logical works of Aristotle in Boethius's translations; Virgil; Pliny; Martianus Capella, on whose work he wrote a surviving commentary; Macrobius; the pseudo-Augustinian *The Ten*

---

1. John gave himself the name "Eriugena" in the preface to his commentary on the *Celestial Hierarchy*. On the names given to John see Cappuyns, *Erigène*, 3–7.

2. Ibid., 9.

3. See ibid., 66–67; Edwards, *Christian Ireland*, 591.

Categories; and Christian authors such as Origen (in Rufinus's translation), Marius Victorinus, Boethius, Ambrose, and, most of all, Augustine. What truly distinguished him from many of his contemporaries, however, was his knowledge of Greek, which gave him access to such Christian Neoplatonists as Gregory of Nyssa, pseudo-Dionysius the Areopagite, and Maximus the Confessor.[4] One also should not overlook the influence of his Irish roots on his unique manner of adapting his sources.[5] His natural gifts and rich education produced a man who was a scholar, teacher, poet, and mystic—the ideal Carolingian Renaissance man.

"It would not be inappropriate to say that if the reign of Charlemagne was the springtime of the Carolingian renaissance, the reign of Charles the Bald was its glorious summer."[6] Every genius is in debt to the circumstances that allow him to flourish and undoubtedly Eriugena owed much to the remarkable environment that nourished him. Though internecine conflicts marred the lands ceded to the grandsons of Charlemagne (742–814)—Lothar (795–855), Pippin (797–838), Louis the German (806–76), and Charles the Bald (823–77)—the intellectual and cultural revival would continue to find patrons among them. Charles, in particular, fostered the talent that entered his fold—even when it came from shadowy lands in the West.

Charles was the son of Louis the Pious's (778–840) second wife, Judith, which made him an outsider from the beginning. Though he received an excellent education—he was most likely fluent in several languages, including Latin—and he acquired a superb formation for ruling, his half-brothers, at least at first, could not but perceive him as an intruder.[7] In fact, it was Louis the Pious's desire to give Charles a portion of the kingdom in 832 that, in part, triggered years of fraternal conflict. A formal resolution was found in the treaty of Verdun in 843, which partitioned the kingdom

---

4. On Eriugena's formation and sources see Carabine, *Eriugena*, 20–22; Moran, "Origen and Eriugena"; Moran, *Philosophy*, 103–22; Sheldon-Williams, "Sources." Willemien Otten notes, in particular, Eriugena's desire unify the Eastern and Western traditions of patristic thought: "He does so not only by assembling what are merely separate parts but by ambitiously suggesting if not proving that a continuous tradition must rationally have preceded its unfortunate fragmentation into scattered parts." Otten, "Texture," 43.

5. For instance, regarding the influence of Irish art on Eriugena's thought see Richardson, "Themes," 280.

6. Jeauneau, "Pseudo-Dionysius," 138.

7. On Charles's education and formation see Nelson, *Charles the Bald*, 85–89; "Reign," 2.

among Louis, Lothar, and Charles. Thus the Western lands that make up modern France became the primary fields for Charles's reign.[8]

Peace did not bless Charles's rule for any length of time—he faced on-going tensions with his family and rebellion from the Bretons, among others; but he was resilient and would live to be crowned emperor by Pope John VIII in 875, two years before his death. During his reign he worked diligently to increase the prestige of the monarchy and promoted the union between church and state.[9] This included the support of education and cultural initiatives, as well as the reception and absorption of learning from the Greek-speaking world.[10] His merits would earn encomiums from his beneficiaries that, though unsurprisingly sycophantic, nonetheless reflect some genuine gratitude and esteem. Eriugena himself could sing—in Greek!—his praises:

> O Charles, Orthodox king! Pious and renowned ruler!
> The Christ-bearer! Prudent Lord![11]

Eriugena came to the continent perhaps out of necessity—the Viking raids were forcing numerous exiles to seek safer havens—perhaps out of the desire for support and inspiration in the celebrated intellectual milieus of the Carolingian world.[12] Though one may connect Eriugena with the Palace School of Charles the Bald, he appears to have also had associations with other centers, including Rheims, Soissons, and Laon.[13] He would enter the fertile environment of the Carolingian revival that engaged scholars from throughout Europe—Irish, Italians, Franks, and others—in the editing of texts, the recovery of sources, and even theological discussions.[14]

---

8. Yet this hardly means that Charles can be called "the founder" of modern France. For a critique of idea see Nelson, *Charles the Bald,* 1–4.

9. On Charles's attempts to magnify his rule see Schieffer, "Regno," 14–15. Charles himself became the Abbot of the prestigious monastery of San Denis in 867. See McKitterick, "Palace School," 330.

10. Michael McCormick outlines some of the ways that Greek learning entered the West during this period, including contacts with Greek monasteries in Rome, the Frankish presence in Jerusalem, and movement through diplomatic channels. See McCormick, "Diplomacy."

11. *Carm.* II, 66, 67–68.

12. A large number of Irish scholars became prominent figures in many ecclesiastical circles during the Carolingian rule. See Edwards, *Christian Ireland,* 591–92; Contreni, "The Irish 'Colony.'"

13. See McKitterick, "Palace School," 327; O'Meara, *Eriugena,* 13–14.

14. See Moran, *Philosophy,* 7–16.

In fact, it was in the heat of theological debate that Eriugena first becomes known. The monk Gottschalk of Orbais (808–867) had sparked a long-running controversy surrounding his affirmation of "double predestination"—God predestines persons both to heaven and hell—that entangled some of the great luminaries of the day, including Hrabanus Maurus (780–856) and Hincmar (806–82), bishop of Rheims. Much of the debate involved interpretations of Augustine, the use of patristic florilegia, and even the application of syllogistic and dialectical reasoning.[15] Hincmar himself would invite Eriugena to refute Gottschalk in 852, with mixed results (see below). Yet the Irishman would leave his mark through his attention to the sources and innovative use of dialectic.

From his first appearance, one must map out his life primarily through the signposts of his scholarship. He became a successful and respected teacher within the palace school, meriting a special charge from Charles himself: the translation of the Dionysian corpus housed in the monastery of San Denis (see below). He completed this project between 860–62 and went on to translate other church fathers into Latin. Thus began the period of his "Greek awakening" that would so profoundly shape his output in the years ahead.

In the remaining years of the decade he wrote his most significant work, *The Periphyseon*, which he apparently revised and annotated even into the 870s.[16] His *Commentary to the Gospel of John, Homily on the Prologue on John* and his poetry were also written during this period. The poem *Aulae sidereae*, which most likely celebrates the consecration of the church of St. Mary in Compiègne in 877, is the latest work in the Eriugenian corpus.[17] Most scholars, therefore, establish his death in the late 870s or early 880s.

Unverifiable legends contribute to the mystery of Eriugena, especially the story of his demise. It was said that his own students stabbed him to death with their styli in response to his unorthodox ideas. More likely a cautionary tale for radical professors than a historical account, it still holds

---

15. "The debate concerned the very nature of learning itself, fuelled by Gottshcalk's use of the syllogism, the result of inspiration during his reading of Jerome on Galatians, and polarized by Eriugena's use of dialectic which drew on Augustine's early dialogue." Ganz, "Debate," 284. Also see Marenbon, "John Scottus," 305; d'Onofrio, *Fons scientiae*, 280–84.

16. On the manuscripts and the questions surrounding the annotations see Moran, *Philosophy*, 60–64.

17. *Carm.* XXV, 116–21.

allegorical merit: in the history of thought, councils have condemned him[18] and students have too long ignored him. It is time to resurrect his voice and spirit through the treasures that he left behind.

Works

Translations

Eriugena's translations alone, despite their limitations, earn him an important place in Western intellectual history. These works also proved most formative for the translator, since they introduced him to the Proclean strand of Neoplatonism and to the rich ideas of the patristic East.[19] Furthermore, Eriugena developed a new vocabulary in order to convey the foreign concepts to his Western readers.[20]

At the behest of Charles the Bald, he prepared a Latin version of the Dionysian Corpus, a collection of works by a mysterious fifth-century Christian Neoplatonist.[21] The Greek manuscript of the corpus had arrived in the monastery of San Denis in 827 as a gift to Louis the Pious from the Byzantine Emperor, Michael II (770–829), and was greatly valued by the Carolingians, since many claimed that its purported author—St. Paul's convert, Dionysius the Areopagite (Acts 17:34)—was the founding Bishop of Paris.[22] The Abbot Hilduin had already attempted a translation, but its inadequacies prompted Charles to seek a better version. Eriugena's translation would have great success, despite the backhanded compliment by the esteemed Anastasius the Librarian (810–78) in Rome, who marveled that a "barbarian from the ends of the world" could accomplish such a task.[23]

Anastasius was gracious enough to send corrections to the manuscript that also included excerpts from the commentary attributed to the

---

18. For instance, *The Periphyseon* was condemned for its connection with the Amalrician heresy at the beginning of the thirteenth century. See Cappuyns, *Erigène*, 247–48.

19. See Meyendorff, "Remarks," 53–58; Cappuyns, *Erigène*, 146–79.

20. See Moran, *Philosophy*, 54.

21. These works include *The Divine Names, The Celestial Hierarchy, The Ecclesial Hierarchy,* and *The Mystical Theology,* as well as a collection of letters. For excellent overviews of the corpus, its origins, and its content see Lilla, *Dionigi l'Areopagita,* 159–97; Rorem, *Pseudo-Dionysius.*

22. On the importance of Dionysius in Carolingian culture see Riché, "Charles le Chauve," 41–42.

23. Arnaldi, "Anastasio Bibliotecario," 519.

seventh-century monk, Maximus the Confessor. These annotations would inspire Eriugena to seek out the works of the great theologian-martyr and to translate them into Latin. He would follow with translations of Gregory of Nyssa's *On the Making of Man*, a work that would have a profound impact upon Eriugena's anthropology, and the *Ancoratus* of Epiphanius of Salamis.[24]

Original Works

As already noted, Eriugena burst onto the scene during the controversy surrounding the question of predestination. The charges against Gottschalk had already been laid out by Hincmar of Reims, Hrabanus Maurus, and others: Gottschalk's "double-predestination" made God responsible for evil, denied human free will, and turned God into an unjust judge.[25] Hincmar would call Eriugena in for reinforcement—and would live to regret it. The Irishman's *De praedestinatione* fell prey to criticism from both parties in the debate. In a controversy that raged around the interpretation of biblical texts, the writings of St. Augustine, and compilations of patristic florilegia, Eriugena's use of dialectic and non-Christian sources shocked his contemporaries.[26] Furthermore, certain positions—such as the idea that God does not punish, but rather that sinners will punish themselves through the perverse direction of their wills—seemed to deviate from certain teachings of Augustine. The work would receive its own condemnation in the council of Valence in 855.

The influence of his encounters with Greek learning, however, would bear greater fruit in the production of his masterpiece, the *Periphyseon*, or *The Division of Nature*, composed between 860–66. It is a dazzling achievement, an original synthesis of Western—particularly Augustinian—and Eastern learning that has defied scholarly categorization.[27] Its very exis-

24. For a reconstruction of Eriugena's pursuit of manuscripts and Greek learning see Jeaneau, "Pseudo-Dionysius," 140–43; O'Meara, *Eriugena*, 51–79.

25. Marenbon, "John Scottus," 305.

26. Prudentius of Troyes, for instance, noted that Jerome had been chastised for his love of Cicero and that, therefore, Eriugena should not have been so reliant upon fallible human reason. See Ganz, "The Debate," 293. Also see Carabine, *John Scottus Eriugena*, 9–12; d'Onofrio, *Fons scientiae*, 283.

27. "Conflicting tendencies seem to underlie this work, as it displays not only an eclectic configuration of topics but also an unusual variety of genres. Such conflicting tendencies have complicated the analysis of the *Periphyseon* as an original and important

tence challenges the canard that the ninth-century West belonged to "the Dark Ages."

The *Periphyseon* is a dialogue between a master (the *Nutritor*) and his pupil (the *Alumnus*), and Eriugena organizes the five books of the discussion around the four divisions of nature: a) that which creates and is not created (God source of all things); b) that which is created and creates (the primordial causes in the Word); c) that which is created and does not create (the created effects); d) that which neither creates nor is created (God as final cause—a topic that required the last two books for its treatment).[28] These divisions, Eriugena notes, should not deceive us into thinking that nature genuinely consists in such radical divides, since the distinctions in fact emerge from the limitations of fallen human cognition. In the end, he demonstrates that all of creation is God's "self-creation": a movement from God as non-being, that is, divine independence and incomprehensibility, to created theophanies (*exitus*); and a return of all things from diversity to unity in God (*reditus*). In creation there is a unity in diversity and a diversity in unity, in which God, as creator and end (divisions one and four), and creation, as causes and effects (divisions two and three), find a resolution in the eternal, divine desire that "all may be one." As Willamien Otten notes, "From the fact that all things are meant to be reduced to the omnipotent source of their derivative existence, we can infer that the purpose of this fourfold division is clearly no other than to channel *natura* through the process of its unfolding into multiplicity towards its final rest in the indivisible God."[29]

What was startling for Eriugena's contemporaries, and even for subsequent generations, was the radically new approach that he had acquired from his reading of Augustine and his Greek sources. Eduard Jeauneau points toward the significance of this accomplishment when he writes that, "while Augustine was indebted to the older form of Neoplatonism, that represented by Plotinus and Porphyry, Dionysius is indebted to a later form, represented by Proclus. For the first time in the history of human thought the two Neoplatonic streams converged. And they converged in a mind widely open, qualified to combine them harmoniously."[30] Later

---

work in the history of Christian thought." Otten, "Eriugena's *Periphyseon*," 69.

28. See *Peri.* I, 3–4, 19–26. On possible sources for the divisions see Carabine, *Eriugena*, 30–31.

29. Otten, *Anthropology*, 26.

30. Jeauneau, "Neoplatonic Themes," 8. On the influence of both strands of

charges of heresy on account of *Periphyseon*'s seeming pantheism failed to understand some of the features of Eriugena's innovative synthesis, particularly the notion of God as non-being, which separated the divine from the category of dependent creature. As we shall see, the *Periphyseon* also offers an important framework for understanding the Incarnation, the descent of the Word into the fragmented state of created effects.

Other surviving works reveal further talents in the Irishman. He proved himself to be an adept scriptural commentator in his *Homily on the Prologue to the Gospel of John* and the remaining portions of his *Commentary on the Gospel of John*, in which he made great use of the Greek text.[31] Commentaries on pseudo-Dionysius's *Celestial Hierarchy* and Martianus Capella's *On the Marriage of Philology and Mercury* established him as an important expositor of seminal thinkers.

Finally, his poetry—in both Latin and Greek—is at last finding a deserved audience among contemporary theologians and philosophers.[32] The *Carmina* embrace a variety of themes: praise for Charles the Bald and Queen Irmintrudis, hymns for Easter and the Harrowing of Hell, even a complaint over the low quality of beverages for exiled Irishmen.[33] Its value for the study of Christology will be proven during the course of this study.

We are fortunate to have critical editions of Eriugena's major works and translations. Now it is up to scholars and readers to discover the many riches that they offer.[34]

Neoplatonism and the question of direct contact with Neoplatonic authors see Moran, *Eriugena*, 105–7.

31. Ludwig Bieler offers some important reflections on Eriugena's use of Greek in interpreting the Latin version. See Bieler, "Observations," 235–39.

32. "Not only do the *Carmina* reflect Eriugena's philosophical and theological concerns, but they contain precious information about his life and his reaction to contemporary history." Dutton, "Eriugena," 51. Also see Colnago, *Poesia e teologia*.

33. "Bacchus abest siccis Scottorum faucibus estu
Et ventres nostros morbida replet aqua."
Carm. XIX, 104, 1–2.

34. Questionable writings—such as the remaining fragments of a commentary on the Gospel of Matthew—and spurious works remain objects of study. See Sheldon-Williams, "List of Works," 66–98; Piemonte, "Distinctive Theses."

Assessments of Eriugena's Christology

Eriugena's works received positive commentary, as well as condemnations, in his own century,[35] and one can trace the influence of his ideas throughout the Middle Ages and Renaissance in such authors as Robert Grosseteste, Thomas Aquinas, and, above all, Meister Eckhart and Nicholas of Cusa.[36] His thought—particularly in its idealist tendencies—also found resonances in the modern period, prompting H. von Schubert to write, "This Irishman has been rightly considered the initiator of an evolution which was not recovered until modern time. He holds a place between Plato-Origen-Dionysius and Spinoza-Fichte-Hegel."[37] Today he finds admirers particularly among critics of onto-theology, who seek to recover the fruits of Christian apophaticism.[38]

There exist, however, few assessments of Eriugena's Christology. While most general surveys of his work acknowledge the importance of Christ for initiating the return of all things, few delve any further into the nuances of his teaching. The resulting evaluations are mixed.

The strongest critics of his Christology generally focus upon four issues. First, they claim that Eriugena overlooks the historical Jesus in favor of his radically intellectualist view of reality. Marcia Colish writes, "For John, Christ acts as the redeemer of man less through what he did on earth than through what he was. As the incarnate God, the nexus between matter and spirit, Christ is the archetype of the creation and the means by which it returns to its divine source. For man this process of return is an essentially contemplative one."[39] Eriugena's Christology, therefore, takes little account of Jesus's historical existence and the potential for Christian imitation of his life.

Second, his Christology lacks the rich sense of the effective synergism of the hypostatic union that one finds in such church fathers as Maximus the Confessor. While the reciprocity between the divine and human

---

35. The problem of glosses in the manuscripts of the *Periphyseon*—which may include annotations and additions from Eriugena himself—made the preparation of a critical edition a difficult challenge. See Greetham, "Jeauneau's Edition."

36. See Moran, *Philosophy*, 269–81.

37. Quoted in Cappuyns, *Erigène*, 267.

38. Wayne Hankey, however, has been extremely critical of this "postmodern" retrieval of the Neoplatonic tradition. See Hankey, "Misrepresenting Neoplatonism"; "The Postmodern Retrieval."

39. Colish, "Christology," 138. Also see Duclow, "Dialectic," 116.

natures, united in the person of Jesus, is the basis for creation's deification[40] in Maximus, this notion seems to be lacking in Eriugena. This results in a form of monophysitism, in which created nature functions only as a passive framework for the return.[41]

Third, critics assert that Eriugena does not take into account the sacramental, ecclesial, and ethical dimensions of the Incarnation of the Word. This weakness makes him a traitor particularly to his Greek sources, which developed all of the dimensions of the Word-made-flesh.[42] Thus, Eriugena's thought finds itself often tainted by gnostic tendencies.

Finally, his thought generally excludes the centrality of Christ that one finds in the Fathers. Though his "rather inchoate Christology"[43] acknowledges the importance of the Incarnation for the redemption of fallen creation, it does not see the *incarnate* Word as the basis for God's creative act itself. The Incarnation is not the central point for God's relation with the world.[44]

This does not mean that Eriugena lacks his defenders. Numerous books and articles have touched upon his diphysite Christology,[45] his references to the sacraments and the church,[46] his understanding of the historical import of the Incarnation,[47] and even the centrality of the Incarnation

40. Deification—θέωσις or *deificatio*—is the traditional doctrine that man will be so perfectly united with the Creator that he will become "divine," without loosing the integrity of his own nature. On deification in antiquity see Russell, *Deification*.

41. See Perl, "Metaphysics," 262–63; Meyendorff, "Remarks," 61.

42. See Colish, "Christology," 139; Duclow, "Dialectic," 116.

43. Carabine, *Eriugena*, 98.

44. This negative assessment is generally accompanied by a comparison with Maximus the Confessor. "In Eriugena, the doctrine of the Incarnation remains distinct from, although closely connected with, his Neoplatonic account of the world's procession from and return to God. It is rather in St. Maximus, the heir of both Neoplatonic metaphysics and Byzantine Christology, that we find the complete union, or rather identification of the two. Maximus offers, not only an idea of a 'cosmic Christ', but a fully integrated Christological ontology, in which the mystery of Christ is itself the basis for understanding the metaphysics of the relation between God and world." Perl, "Metaphysics," 153. Also see Meyendorff, "Remarks," 61–62.

45. For instance see Ansorge, *Wahrheit*, 322–32; Cappuyns, *Erigène*, 363; Mooney, *Theophany*, 175–76; Rorem, *Eriugena's Commentary*, 146, 158–59.

46. For instance see McEvoy, "Reditus," 376; McGinn, "Eriugena Mysticus," 250; Walker "Erigena's Conception," 157.

47. For instance see Jeauneau, "Themes," 20–21; Jeauneau, "Ambigua," 90; Moran, "Idealism," 76.

in his thought.[48] Yet these treatments are generally all too brief assessments lost within other arguments. Eriugena's Christology demands a closer examination and evaluation.

The Scope of This Book

This book examines the significance of the Incarnation in Eriugena's thought. On the one hand, it may be called a defense. His major critics have undervalued Eriugena's creative appropriation of the tradition, as well as the overall importance of the Word-made-flesh in his works. A proper assessment demands a wider examination of the sources—for instance, his poetry and scriptural commentaries—and a proper consideration of the Incarnation in the context of these sources. The understanding of the Incarnation that emerges from this study should adequately refute some of the harsher critiques that the Irishman has suffered.

On the other hand, this volume is a modest introduction. For those new to Eriugena, the Incarnation offers an excellent thematic entry into the world of this fascinating and stimulating thinker. For those who are already familiar with his thought, this book should provide a new perspective and, hopefully, inspiration for further research. It in no way purports to be the exhaustive or definitive study—the conclusion will indicate further important avenues for scholars. It lives in the hope that others will respond—positively and negatively—with renewed vigor toward the study of Eriugena's vision.

This book contends that, in fact, Eriugena's understanding of the Incarnation provides a form of free participation in God that includes the mystical appropriation of the historical life of the Word. In examining the Incarnation, one comes to see the importance of humanity's free, personal cooperation with God in the redemption and elevation of the cosmos. It has the following plan: first, an examination of embodiment and the flesh in Eriugena's thought; second, a consideration of his appropriation of the tradition in his treatment of the Incarnation; third, a summary of the "motives" behind the Word becoming flesh; fourth, a presentation of the anthropological basis for humanity's participation in the divine; and finally, a treatment of Eriugena's notion of *imitatio Christi*, rooted in the genuine historical and physical reality of the incarnate Christ.

---

48. For instance see Beierwaltes, *Eriugena*, 187; Carabine, "Virgins," 197; Jeauneau, "Pseudo-Dionysius," 148.

1

Being Human, Being Flesh

ERIUGENA DECLARES THAT THE WORD "was made fully man, subsisting in flesh, soul and mind."[1] Yet before considering the significance of the Incarnation in his thought, we must carefully qualify what the Word assumed in becoming flesh. Since flesh, as this chapter will show, designates a particular *state* of the human body after the fall, to say that the Word became incarnate means that God actually entered into humanity's world of suffering and death.

This chapter follows the fall of humanity into the tragic state of material existence. First, it examines the reasons behind humanity's creation. Second, it considers humanity's embodied state in paradise, that is, the prelapsarian spiritual body. Finally, it takes up the problem of the fleshly state after the fall. The journey of this chapter, therefore, takes a tragic course that concludes in a world of suffering, instability, and decay. Yet the flesh also contains the hope of restoration and elevation in the Incarnation of the Word. "Where man reaches the end of his Fall, there begins his return."[2]

Before proceeding, it should be noted that Eriugena's allegorical reading of the Scriptures, particularly his reading of *Genesis*, often challenges modern sensibilities. Like the ancient exegetes before him, he understood the hermeneutical difficulties in explaining the creation story with its disturbing anthropomorphisms, repetitions, and inconsistencies. Though the

1. *Peri.* IV, 6, 102–13.

2. ". . . ubi ruinae suae finem posuit, inde iterum redire inchoavit." *Peri.* V, 23, 663–64.

resources of the historical-critical method were obviously not available to him, he did overcome these obstacles through an allegorical interpretation of the narrative that sought to penetrate the deeper mysteries of humanity's tragic circumstances and hunger for liberation. The text of God's Word remained ever his guide, since even its problems inspired contemplation of the mysteries of the fall and redemption. Perhaps Leon Kass's words regarding the reading of *Genesis*—and the reading of the Scriptures in general—will open the contemporary reader to the possibilities of the Irishman's exegesis: "We may be disappointed in the [scriptural] text's lack of clarity, but we are at the same time grateful that the account leaves mysterious what cannot help but be mysterious. In this sense, at least, we believe that the text tells the truth: we already suspect that there is no way for us human beings to visualize clearly or to understand fully the awesome coming into being of the world. We begin to trust the text."[3]

The Reasons for Creation

The Glory of God

Why did God create and what is humanity's vocation within the divine plan? In general, Eriugena gives three reasons for God's creative act. First, he states that "all things were created out of nothing in order that the breadth and bounty of divine goodness might be manifested and praised through the things which he made."[4] Things come to be for God's greater glory. In the act of creation, God "makes" and reveals himself, since he moves from the darkness of non-being—the incomprehensible and transcendent divinity—into the light of intelligible being in things that he makes.

This creative act also demands intelligent beings that may know and praise God. God's greater glory comes from the free response of angels and men:

> If the divine Goodness had remained alone in itself, at rest and without action, it perhaps would not have created an occasion for its praise. But now [the divine Goodness], pouring itself out into all visible and invisible things, and existing as all things and in all things, turns the rational and intellectual creature toward knowledge of itself. Thus, God made everything in order to show every

3. Kass, "The Beginning," 29.
4. *Peri.* V, 128, 4126–27.

rational and intellectual creature the innumerable and beautiful
species of the rest of creation as material for his praise. He did this
that there might not be any creature that does not, either through
itself or in itself or through another, praise the Supreme Good.[5]

Intellectual creatures—angels and men—glorify God by knowing
God's self-manifestation in creation and by praising him through that
knowledge.

Divine Fecundity

A second general reason for creation comes from the very notion of divine
Goodness: Goodness itself is inherently fecund.[6] God emerges from the
impregnability of divine non-being through an act of natural generosity
and love: "The Highest Good, which is a subsisting Good from itself and
in itself, must not abstain from the creation (*conditio*) of goods, which are
good neither from themselves nor in themselves, but from the Good itself
and in the Good itself. For this reason he created existing things from non-
existence, lest he be reproached for jealousy by holding himself back from
the establishment (*substitutio*) of those things that he was able to establish
(*substituere*)."[7] This divine abundance that pours forth into creation does
not imply an unwilled act, but rather it reveals God's free outflowing generosity and majesty.[8]

---

5. *Peri.* V, 128, 4134–44.

6. This is a central teaching of Neoplatonism. "Now when anything else comes to
perfection we see that it produces, and does not endure to remain by itself, but makes
something else." Plotinus, *Enneades* V, iv, i, 143. Gustavo Piemonte notes that Eriugena's
use of images of the "diffusion" of the divine distinguishes an act of a demiurge from a
genuine act of creation, in which creation depends upon the Good from which it comes.
See Piemonte, "Image," 91–94. Also see Wallis, *Neoplatonism,* 61–66.

7. *Peri.* V, 128, 4145–50.

8. God's will is free and he does not create out of compulsion. "For if the will of God
is free—and it is impious to believe otherwise—truly his free will lacks any necessity, and
therefore no necessity possesses the will of God." *Prae.* II, i, 10, 20–23. On the question
of divinely willed or natural emanation in both non-Christian and Christian authors see
Gersh, *From Iamblicus,* 18–23; Jeauneau, "Themes," 12–13.

Love

God creates because God is love: "It is right, therefore, that God is said to be love, because he is the cause of all love, and he is diffused through all things, and he gathers all things into one, and it turns back to him in an ineffable return. He encloses the loving motions of the whole of creation in himself. Also, the diffusion itself of the divine nature into all things, which are in the divine nature and come from it, is called the love of all things."[9] Since creation is a theophany of the divine—God "makes" himself, that is, he comes to be known in what he creates—it comes "to be" as an expression of perfect divine love. Creation remains distinct from God because it cannot be its own cause and origin; yet it remains ever united with the Creator through the bond of charity, since, "love is a connection and chain, with which the totality of all things is joined by an ineffable friendship and indissoluble unity."[10]

Eriugena adopts the passionate words of Maximus the Confessor to describe the love of God that creates and unifies all things: "God moves and is moved, as one thirsting to be thirsted for, loving to be loved, and desiring to be desired."[11] God creates out of love, but God also desires to be loved in return.

Humanity's Role in God's Creation

Man holds a central role in the cosmos, since he is the knower who effectively bestows being upon the causes of creation. To understand this notion, it is first necessary to examine some principles that Eriugena draws from his sources, in particular from pseudo-Dionysius and Augustine.

The Theophany of the Super-essential God

Eriugena inherits and adapts a Neoplatonic tradition that equates being with intelligibility and thought.[12] The true essence of a thing cannot be in matter or sensible bodies, since matter is in constant flux and decay. Thus, Plotinus, for instance, states that something can "be" only if it shares in

9. *Peri.* I, 107, 3329–34.
10. *Peri.* I, 106, 3304–6.
11. *Peri.* I, 108, 3364–65. Quoting Maximus, *Ambigua* XIX, 1260C.
12. See Garcia, "Ontological Characterization," 160.

definable limitations outside of sense experience that allow it to be conceived: "Being must not fluctuate, so to speak, in the indefinite, but must be fixed by limit and stability; and stability in the intelligible world is limitation and shape, and it is by these that it receives existence."[13] That which *is* must be comprehensible, to the point that one may identify being and thought. Eric Perl notes that "Plotinus, far more explicitly than Plato, identifies being not only as the object but as the content of thought and therefore as Thought, or Intellect, itself. For . . . if being were external to thought, then the actual content of thought, what thought apprehends, would not be reality itself but some image or impression of it."[14]

In this Neoplatonic tradition, the Cause of being—in the sense that all beings refer to it as their cause—cannot be classified as being itself. In fact, it cannot be classified at all, since it transcends all definition or intelligible notions. This cause, the One, may rightfully be called "non-being," not because it does not "exist" or is not "real," but rather because it cannot be rendered intelligible by limiting categories and does not belong to the universe of those categories. One must never conceive of the One as just another object, but it is better to respect the divine darkness in its mystery. Proclus, for instance, states that the Cause of all being is itself the unqualified and uncaused Good, that is, the One who is beyond comprehension and participation.[15]

The Christian Neoplatonist who assumed the name of Dionysius the Areopagite also developed this apophatic approach to God by adopting the Neoplatonic notion of saying that God is "beyond being" or is "non-being." God is "not" in the sense of his ineffability or incomprehensibility: "For if all knowledge is of beings and is limited to beings, then that which is beyond being is outside of knowledge."[16] God is *hyperousios*, beyond any categorization or essence.[17]

---

13. Plotinus, *Enneades* V, i, *vii*, 37. Also see Proclus, *Institutio*, Prop. LXXXIX, 83.

14. Perl, *Theophany*, 9.

15. "If unification is in itself good, and all good tends to create unity, then the unqualified Good and the unqualified One merge into a single principle, a principle which makes things one and in doing so makes them good." Proclus, *Institutio*, Prop. XIII, 17. "For in the first place, it is clear that the One is imparticipable; were it participated, it would thereby become the unity of a particular and cease to be the cause both of existent things and of the principles prior to existence." Proclus, *Institutio*, Prop. CXVI, 103.

16. Dionysius, *De divinis nominibus* I, iv, 115, 16–18.

17. For instance see Dionysius, *De divinis nominibus* II, iv, 126, 14–17; 127, 1–7.

Following these principles regarding divine incomprehensibility, Eriugena speaks of creation *ex nihilo* as God's creation from himself, that is, from his ineffable non-being. God, as the cause of all being, cannot be classified among beings: "Essence, therefore, may be predicated of God, but he is not essence in the proper sense. . . . Therefore he is *hyperousios*, that is, superessential."[18] Yet in God's creative act, he becomes, in a limited sense, manifest and intelligible in created being: God moves from *nothing* (that is, non-being) to *something* intelligible (that is, being). Creation itself is a theophany, a descent of the unintelligible, super-essential Creator into intelligible being:

> Then, from the superessentiality of his nature, in which he is said not to be, [God] descends first in the primordial causes and he creates himself. And he becomes the beginning of every essence, every life, every intelligence, and of all things that gnostic contemplation considers in the primordial causes. Next, from the primordial causes, which hold a certain mediating position between God and creation (that is, between the ineffable superessentiality beyond every intellect and nature that is substantially manifest and perceptible to pure minds), he descends and is made in the effects of these things. He is revealed manifestly in his theophanies. Then he moves through the multiple forms of the effects to the last rank of nature, in which bodies are contained.[19]

God is the source of the primordial causes of all things and, in turn, of all the effects that stem from them. God, therefore, comes to be "made" in creation by becoming comprehensible: he is known and therefore "is" in the created cosmos.

Man as the Primordial Knower and Field of Creation

Eriugena takes the radical position that all things eternally exist in the Word, the second person of the Trinity: "If therefore the Word of God itself

---

18. *Peri.* I, 28, 748–50. Paul Blowers notes that this understanding of *creatio ex nihilo* affirms not only divine apophaticism, but also divine giftedness: "In the end, Eriugena, while developing his theology of creation . . . is absolutely at one with Dionysius and Maximus on the principle that the divine 'nothing,' apart from being the focus of an intense apophaticism, also inspires deep wonder at the Creator's incomprehensible love, his ecstatic and indeed 'incarnational' descent through the eternal *causae* (or *logoi*) to the being and 'well-being' of created things." Blowers, *Drama*, 183–84.

19. *Peri.* III, 91, 2639–50.

makes all things and is made in all things . . . why should one marvel if all things, which are understood to subsist in the Word itself, are believed and are known to be eternal and made at the same time?"[20] He supports this position on the ground that the primordial causes of all things cannot be accidents of God, since God is simple, that is, God cannot be defined by parts that are distinguishable from himself. Logically, this means that the causes are not only "co-eternal" with the Word, but also they *are* the Word. In the Word, the causes are one within the divine darkness; only in creation are they perceived as multiple. Thus the Word is both one in himself, and multiple in his diffusion in created things: "The simple and in itself infinitely multiple creative Reason and Cause of the created universe is the Word of God. Or, to put it another way: The Word of God is the simple and, in himself, infinitely multiple creative Reason and Cause of the created universe."[21] The Truth of creation, therefore, is the Word, since there is a perfect unity between the knower—Christ, the Word—and known—the primordial causes of all things.[22]

The primordial causes in the Word remain within the inscrutable darkness of non-being and, therefore, do not come "to be" in their multiplicity until they are received and known by one other than the Word, that is, by a *created* knower, or, in Eriugena's term, "created wisdom." When creation is known in the Word, it is indistinguishable from him; when creation comes to be known by a created knower, it comes to be in its effects. Who is this created knower? At this point, Eriugena finds his answer through an adaptation of a teaching from Augustine of Hippo.

In his *De Genesi ad litteram*, Augustine posits that the hexaemeron took place in the created intellect of the angels. The angels, created with the light,[23] become the privileged knowers in whom creation first takes place:

20. *Peri.* III, 41, 1156–59.

21. *Peri.* III, 36, 983–87.

22. See Moran, *Philosophy*, 135. Moran develops his argument in part from a passage in *Periphyseon* II, which appears to be the addition of a commentator (i2): *Christus qui omnia intelligit, immo est omnium intellectus.* Yet Eriugena's position on Christ as the Creative Wisdom adds support to the idea of Christ as the eternal intellect. "For the essence of all things is nothing else than the knowledge of all things in the divine Wisdom." *Peri.* II, 45, 1058–59. Compare with Plotinus, *Enneades* V, ix, viii, 307: "Being and Intellect are therefore one nature; so therefore are the real beings and the active actuality of being and Intellect of this kind; and the thoughts of this kind are the form and shape of being and its active actuality."

23. "And the reason God said, 'Let light be made,' and light was made (Gen 1:3), was so that what was there in the Word might be here in the actual work. The fashioning of

"For through the course of all six days, when those things which God was pleased to establish one by one were being established, was not [the angel] receiving first these things in the word of God, in order that they might 'become' first in his [the angel's] knowledge, when it was being said: 'And thus it has been made' (Gen 1:3)?"[24] In the words of Aimé Solignac, Augustine, in this passage, "makes the angelic nature the mirror and the privileged witness of creation, to the point of saying that creation is first made in some fashion in the spirit of the angel. . . . The angelic nature becomes in this way the archetype, the consciousness, and the ideal of the condition of creation."[25] In short, the angels give this creation being when they receive it as created knowers.

Eriugena reshapes Augustine's position by elevating man to the place of the primordial knower. According to the Irishman, both angels *and* men are created in the light—that is, before all things—and, therefore, both intellectual beings become the privileged knowers of the divine causes within their natures. Man is created by knowing himself and all things in himself:

> For no other reason is the creation of the angels not explicitly stated in the word "light"—it is not said, "Let there be angel," nor "Let us make angel" in the same way as it is written, "Let us make man"—than that we may understand that the creation of man, no less than that of angel, is to be understood in the creation of light. But if man is a participant in the creation of the celestial essence, which is signified by the creation of light, who, among those rightly considering the nature of things, would not conclude that all the things in the narrative after the creation of light are created in man, not only according to his knowledge of them, but also according to their very being.[26]

---

heaven, on the other hand, or the sky, was first in the Word of God in terms of begotten Wisdom, then it was made next in the spiritual creation, that is, in the knowledge of the angels, in terms of the wisdom created in them . . ." Augustinus, *De Genesi ad litteram*, I, viii, *xvi*, 23, 20–23; 24, 1–4 (Hill translation, 199–200). Also see *De civitate Dei* XI, ix, 524, 28–29; 525, 1–6: "For when God said, 'Let there be light' (Gen 1:3), and light was created, then, if we are right in interpreting this as including the creation of the Angels, they immediately became partakers of the eternal light, which is the unchanging Wisdom of God, the agent of God's whole creation and the Wisdom we call the only-begotten Son of God, through whom they themselves and all other things were made."

24. Augustinus, *De Genesi ad litteram* IV, xxi, *xlviii*, 129, 7–10.

25. Solignac, "La connaissance," 653. Also see O'Meara, "'Magnorum virorum,'" 10–11; TeSelle, *Augustine*, 215.

26. *Peri.* IV, 59–60, 1650–60.

By placing the creation of man with that of the angel at the beginning of the *Genesis* narrative, Eriugena is now free to understand the subsequent days of creation as the unfolding of the eternal causes in man. The fact that *Genesis* speaks specifically of man only at the end of the narrative does not pose a problem: "Man is introduced after the narrative of visible creation as the conclusion of all things in order that one might understand that all things, which are said to have been created before him, are understood universally *in him.* . . . Indeed, since he is presented at the end of all the divine works, it is clear that all divine works subsist and are comprehended in him."[27] Man has the mission to possess "the concept of all things that were created equal to him or that come under his rule."[28]

Man, therefore, receives the vocation to be "created wisdom": he gives being to creation by knowing it, and becomes all things by knowing them.[29] He holds a unique relationship with the Word, in whom the creation of the causes subsists from all eternity, since man holds the primacy of place in creation as the knower in whom the hexaemeron unfolds:

> Great and true is the praise of human nature, and more so of the One who wished to create it so! Thus one must also accept in the same way these things regarding his intellect and manner of knowing. For, just as Creative Wisdom—that is, the Word of God—saw all things that are made in it before they came to be, and the vision itself of these things, seen before they were made, is their true, immutable and eternal essence; so created wisdom—that is, human nature—knew all those things that are made in itself, before they were made, and the knowledge itself of these things, known before they were made, is their true and unchanging essence. Therefore, Creative Wisdom's [the Word's] knowledge itself is rightly understood to be the primal, causal essence of every creature; but created wisdom's [man's] knowledge subsists as the secondary essence and the effect of the superior knowledge.[30]

27. *Peri.* IV, 60, 1676–79; 1684–86.

28. *Peri.* IV, 41, 1080–84.

29. "However, despite the gigantic scope of nature, it appears that the human mind, while contained by it like the rest of the world including God, serves as its leading principle. After all, *natura* is the sum total of all that is and that is not, whereby the fundamental difference between being and non-being is based solely on the comprehensive capacities of the human mind. This daring cosmology pivoting on human insight is generally seen as one of the most remarkable and innovative feats of the Periphyseon." Otten, *Anthropology,* 4.

30. *Peri.* IV, 55, 1505–18. Also see *Peri.* IV, 41, 1093–1102.

In this passage, Eriugena carefully distinguishes the manner in which essences subsist in the Word and the manner in which they subsist in humanity. The Word "sees" (*vidit*) all things before they are made, not with conceptual knowledge that renders them beings, but in their still undisclosed mystery as eternal and immutable causes in God. Man, however, "knew" (*cognovit*) these hidden causes of the Word in himself, not as eternal essence, which subsists only in the Word, but in their "true and unchangeable" essence as a secondary effect. Man, created wisdom, assumes the place held by the angels in Augustine's *Genesis* commentary as the created intellect in whom things come to be. Yet he always remains subservient to the Word, Creative Wisdom, who eternally sees the hidden causes of God.

Humanity as the Mediator and Source of Unity

Man's composite nature—body and soul—summarizes and unifies all of creation. Man is the "workshop of all creatures" (*creaturarum omnium officina*), containing the hierarchy of beings in himself:

> In man every creature, both visible and invisible, is created. Therefore, he is said to be the "workshop of all things," since in him all things which come after God are contained. Thus he is customarily called an intermediary. Indeed, since he consists of body and soul, he contains within himself and gathers into unity the extremes that are at a distance from himself—that is, the spiritual and material.[31]

Every possible creature finds its exemplar in humanity: "Indeed man understands like an angel, reasons like a man, feels like an irrational animal, lives like a plant, and subsists in both body and soul. He lacks no creature in himself. For apart from these things, you can find no other creature."[32] No other creature—not even the angels!—unites creation in itself. Only humanity effects the unity of God's glorious cosmos: "Connecting the body from this world and the soul from the other world, he [man] makes one harmonious world. Indeed his body possesses every corporeal nature, but his soul possesses every incorporeal nature. These things, since they are joined together by a single joining, form the entire worldly harmony of man."[33]

31. *Peri.* V, 49, 1517–23.

32. *Peri.* III, 163, 4787–90. Also see Augustinus, *De civitate Dei* XII, xxii, 606, 28; 607, 1–15.

33. *Hom.* XIX, 294–96, 17–21. I accept Jeauneau's observation that "ornatus," in

Humanity, therefore, holds a pivotal place in God's plan. Man bestows being upon things by knowing them and unites all things in himself as the mediator, the "third world": "The third world is that which, as a mediator, connects the higher world of spirits and the lower world of bodies, and makes the two one. It is understood that it is man alone who unites every creature."[34] Jorge Garcia rightly notes that "It is through this doctrine of man as a container of the universe that he [Eriugena] explains the unity of created nature with uncreated nature (that is, God), the creation by and return to God of the created universe, knowledge and its bases, and the Incarnation of Christ."[35]

The mediating position of humanity is also a task. In the end, as we shall see, man serves as the one through whom creation will be deified and made one with God.[36] Through freely willed cooperation with grace, man will pass through the barriers between his qualified existence and the divine darkness for perfect union with God, drawing all things that are known in him into this intimate new life. Where humanity goes, so goes all that is.

Man's Spiritual Body in Paradise

One must distinguish between man's *material* body after the fall and man's *spiritual* body in paradise. Though man, in fact, has only one body, that body exists in these two radically different states.

Eriugena maintains that God originally created man as a composite being in a simultaneous creation: God intended the soul-body composite. The body, though of a lower order than the soul, nonetheless belongs to man's pristine formation. Eriugena's doctrine of man's creation, therefore, avoids any form of soul-body dualism:

> But be careful lest, for these reasons, you begin to conjecture that the creation (*creatio*) of the soul preceded the creation (*conditio*) of the body by some temporal gap. Indeed, the soul precedes the body by its dignity and excellence of nature alone, but not by place and time. For all at once, in one single man, who was made in the image of God, the primordial causes of all men were created in

describing "world," translates the Greek word *kosmos* as the harmonious order of the universe. See *Hom.*, 295–96, n. 4.

34. *Hom.* XIX, 292–94, 12–16.
35. Gracia, "Ontological," 157.
36. On deification see *Peri.* V, 217, 7055–68.

soul and body. For in no way, by some temporal delay, does the essence of the soul precede the essence of the body, nor does the essence of the body precede the essence of the soul.[37]

How, then, did this pre-lapsarian body differ from man's body after the fall? Eriugena offers a summary of the distinguishing characteristics in Book Four of the *Periphyseon*. The spiritual body is, "not the corruptible one after sin, but that which existed before the fault; not the composite and decaying body, but the simple and undivided one; not animal and terrestrial, but the spiritual and celestial; not the body born from two sexes through carnal unions by seeds, but the body produced from a simple nature prior to the transgression."[38]

Before examining some of these characteristics more closely, it should be noted that, though the qualities of the pre- and post-lapsarian bodies differ, one might still perceive a single *identity* of the two bodies. As we shall see, the spiritual body created simultaneously with the soul takes on super-added characteristics (*superadiecta*) after its union with matter in the fall. Embodied man becomes flesh when it loses the original state; yet there is a continuity of identity in the composite nature.[39]

37. *Peri.* II, 76, 1787–95. Also see *Peri.* IV, 83, 2446–48. Eriugena draws especially from Maximus the Confessor in formulating this teaching regarding the simultaneous creation of the body and soul, but the contexts of their teachings differ. While Gregory and Maximus were refuting certain "origenist" interpretations of man's creation (the preexistence and fall of souls into bodies), Eriugena defends man's composite nature within his discussion of the Trinitarian image in the soul. After explaining the different operations of the divine Trinity and the soul's trinity, he realizes that his encomium of the soul's lofty status nearly reduces the body to a mere instrument, or even to a form of punishment. It is at this point he abandons his original question—the comparison between the uncreated Trinity and the created trinity—in order to explain the divinely intended creation of composite man: body and soul *belong* together. See Maximus, *Ambigua* XLII, 1341D; Stephanou, "Coexistence," 308–11.

38. *Peri.* IV, 28, 728–38.

39. Carlos Steel highlights the continuity between the material body and the spiritual body: "Although we have to distinguish the natural and the earthly body, we should not consider them as two different bodies. In fact, there is only one body permanently connected to the soul so as to constitute with it one human nature and substance." Steel, "Return," 58. Also see Jeaneau, "Division," 358.

The Body as Spirit

The pre-lapsarian body is spiritual. Yet how can there be a "spiritual" body? In Book Five of the *Periphyseon*, Eriugena defines body as "anything that is extended in length, width or height, and is either a natural body or a geometrical body."[40] Body, therefore, does not necessarily mean something associated with matter, but it can also be something definable and comprehensible, for example a geometric shape.[41] The true nature of bodies is conceptual spirit, defined by the primordial causes. Even after the fall, man's authentic spiritual body continues to shape him and remains hidden within, waiting to slough off the material characteristics that weigh it down and subject it to decay: "Indeed, the reason (*ratio*)[42] of the body is hidden within each man, into which this earthly and mortal body will transform at the time of the resurrection and in which he will become similar to angelic bodies, when men and angels will be equal."[43]

This pre-lapsarian, spiritual body, therefore, is not accessible to the material senses: no material characteristics adhere to it and render it visible.[44] One may know that this spiritual body exists as the expression of the soul, but one cannot describe it using adjectives from the sensible world.

Incorruptibility

The pre-lapsarian body is incorruptible and immutable. Since this body is divorced from corrupted matter, it cannot be subject to change or decay.

---

40. He distinguishes "body" from "incorporeal" and an intermediate state, which he calls "corporal" (*corporale*): "*Incorporeal* is everything that entirely lacks spatial predicates, as it is entirely lacking matter. *Corporal*, however, is color, shape or similar things, which are not bodies because they are understood in association with bodies, nor are they incorporeal because they always adhere to bodies." *Peri.* V, 33, 995–1002. Also see Petroff, "*Theoriae*," 569–70.

41. "Indeed, in human nature nothing subsists which is not spiritual and intelligible. For even the substance of the body is perfectly intelligible." *Peri.* V, 28, 823–25.

42. Here *ratio* may be understood as the authentic definition of man's spiritual body with all its concomitant characteristics. For example see *Peri.* V, 86, 2736–41.

43. *Peri.* V, 186, 6060–64. Regarding the notion of spiritual body see Petroff, "Spiritual Body," 603–6; Sorabji, *Matter*, 114–16.

44. The celestial body, unlike the material body, lacks a qualitative form adhering to matter: "It is the qualitative form joined to matter that makes the body. When I say 'qualitative form', I mean that which appears to the senses after being taken up by quality and quantity, and is always in flux with the matter that it adheres to." *Peri.* III, 119, 3440–44.

Furthermore, as an image of the soul, it reflects the stability and simplicity of the soul itself: "Not only the form of the soul was made in the image of God, but also the natural form of the body, which imitates the image of the soul. It remains forever incorruptible and immutable."[45]

Eriugena follows this principle to its obvious conclusion by stating that the body remains whole and uncorrupted even after the fall. Eventually the "exterior, or material body, weighed down by sensible qualities, will dissolve into its original immaterial elements, when the authentic interior and spiritual body will emerge unchanged. Thus man never really loses his celestial and invisible body, since it remains hidden within him in union with the soul:

> It is not improper to understand the material and exterior body as a kind of garment for the interior and natural body. For it is moved through times and ages, experiencing its increase and decrease, while the interior body always remains unchanged (*incommutabiliter*) in its [genuine] state. But since the exterior body is also made and superadded by God, the greatness of divine goodness and the infinite providence toward all existents does not want it to perish entirely and fade into nothingness, because it is from providence itself and holds the lowest rank among creatures. . . . It was necessary that the exterior and material body be dissolved into those elements from which it was assumed. But it is not necessary for it to perish, since it is from God. The interior body remains always and is established without change (*incommutabiliter*) in its reasons, according to which with the soul, and in the soul, and for the soul, and because of the soul, it is created.[46]

The spiritual body, therefore, truly "is," since it is not subject to the flux of matter and can only be contemplated by the intellect, not by the material senses. Man's pre-lapsarian body is a body in the truest sense, the authentic and stable element of the composite human being.

Freedom from Sexual Distinctions

One sign of the celestial body's integrity and immutability is its freedom from the division of the sexes. If man had not sinned, human nature would have immediately multiplied in the manner of the angels, without recourse

45. *Peri.* V, 19–20, 538–41.
46. *Peri.* IV, 85–86, 2518–37.

to sexual intercourse.[47] Gender, therefore, does not define the spiritual body.[48] Yet as will be noted later, God allowed the distinction between masculine and feminine in fallen humanity for the sake of procreation and the perpetuation of the species in the material order. The decay and death of the material body called for another means of sustaining the human race. Thus "male" and "female" not only mar the simplicity of the spiritual body, but also manifest the corrupt nature of the mortal body in its continuous cycle of birth and death.[49]

Freedom from Sin and Passions

The spiritual body remains free from sin and the deleterious characteristics of sin. As we shall see, the fall distorted man's very perspective of creation, causing him to see things apart from God and in a fragmented form. The material weight of the fallen body contributes greatly to this shattered vision. Yet in its original state, the spiritual body conformed itself to the higher virtues of the soul.

In particular, Eriugena focuses upon the spiritual body's freedom from the passions. Some passions, such as the spiritual senses of the body, are inherent to human nature and therefore are good.[50] Yet the material body, because of its complex nature, contains unnatural passions that attack the Trinitarian image of the soul and obfuscate man's perception of creation. He offers a list of these disordered passions and explains their general association with the carnal body:

> These passions, however, are the generation from bodies in the same manner of irrational beasts; the increases and decreases of bodies and all their corruptions; the final dissolution of the corporeal structure of all bodies; the irrational motions of the soul, which arise from matter and fly around it. All these things are not part of the original condition of humanity, but are added in the beginning on account of humanity's general sin. Thus the passions will perish at the same time with the matter, which they taint, when the primal condition of humanity itself will be liberated from all

47. *Peri.* IV, 82, 2401–5.

48. On Eriugena's "spiritualization" of the human body in paradise see Jeauneau, "Division," 49.

49. See Maximus, *Thalassium* LXI, 97, 218–22. See also Schönborn, "Plaisir," 283.

50. *Peri.* V, 111, 3562–63.

these and similar passions. The spiritual fire of divine grace and goodness will purge them.[51]

The spiritual body, however, was—and will be—free of these malformations and distractions. Since God, who is free of all passions, created the soul and body in his image, man must also be free of disordered passions in his origins.[52] The pre-lapsarian body is not only free of physical passions—generation, disease, etc.—but also from the interior passions that the association with the flesh causes—the "irrational motions" of the soul. Once again, Eriugena highlights the stability of the divine image in the immaterial body-soul unity prior to the advent of sin.

Imperfection

Finally, it is important to note that the absence of disordered attractions in pre-lapsarian man does not imply that he once lived in a state of perfection or absolute fulfillment. On the one hand, God did create man in goodness and with the potential to grow in virtue. Man, from the beginning, possessed a nature imbued with the possibility of growing in the divine likeness and well-being: "For the highest existing intellectual and comprehensive Good creates for no other reason than that it is appropriate for such a creation to possess well-being."[53] God created man without sin and gave him a nature with the potential for wisdom, prudence, and the elevation to divine union.[54]

On the other hand, this paradisiacal state certainly lacked perfection and absolute stability. Man's fall is proof enough for this: if man had been perfect, he would not have turned from God. Eriugena even goes so far as to imply that, right from the beginning, the likelihood of man's obedience to God was slim. From the moment of his creation, man inclined toward sin: "One must think that man was more foolish and imprudent prior to having sinned, than a seeker of wisdom and prudence. For foolishness and imprudence precede sin."[55]

51. *Peri.* V, 111, 3567–78.

52. *Peri.* V, 111, 3559–62. Also see Maximus, *Thalassium* I, 47, 5–13.

53. *Peri.* IV, 77, 2241–43.

54. Man will pass from his "animal" state in paradise to a higher, spiritual state. See *Prae.* VIII, v, 51, 83–84.

55. *Peri.* V, 215, 6981–84.

Furthermore, man faced the temptations of indifference and false contentment in paradise, preferring the natural goods he had received and never seeking the greater gifts God was offering him. This becomes clear in Eriugena's interpretation of the parable of the wise and foolish virgins (Matt 25:1–13). The foolish virgins represent man's disordered contentment in paradise, when man coveted "the natural goods alone, apart from the ornaments of virtue." The wise virgins, however, symbolize man if he had responded to God's gift of "participation in the highest wisdom and all the virtues," that is, "deification and contemplation of the truth."[56]

The first man, therefore, was far from his divinely intended fulfillment, inclining toward disobedience and a form of false contentment right from the beginning. In one passage in Book Four of the *Periphyseon*, however, Eriugena even assumes the position of Maximus the Confessor, stating that man *never* actually existed in paradise, since he fell at the moment of his creation: "Furthermore, in my opinion, one must refer that praise of the life of man in paradise to his future life, if he had remained obedient, and not to an actually existing life, which he had only begun and did not remain firm in. For if, by chance, he had even remained [in paradise] for a short time, he would necessarily have arrived at a certain perfection."[57]

The fact that paradise was not the state of humanity's fulfillment—it existed only *in potentia*—forces Eriugena to ascend to yet another level in order to find the true definition of man. Man, the composite being of body and soul, must have his true and stable definition beyond the inchoate state of paradise, the truth of which remains hidden within man.[58] Yet before examining this problem, we shall continue the descent in order understand humanity's carnal state.

Man's Fleshly Body after the Fall

Eriugena believed that man, destined to respond freely to God and to ascend to a higher union, never existed even for a moment in the paradise of

56. *Peri.* V, 216, 7001–9.

57. *Peri.* IV, 96, 2845–49. See Maximus, *Thalassium* LXI, 85, 12–16. Also see Larchet, *Divinisation*, 179–80.

58. "Rather than unpacking paradise as mere allegory, however, with the human mind (νοῦς) becoming tragically weighed down by the senses (αἴσθησις), his solution is to cultivate the pardisical garden as an image representing eschatological fulfillment. Paradise, in other words, becomes the cherished site of a dignified humanity before a generous creator." Otten, "Pedagogical Aspect," 520.

his nature as a composite of soul and spiritual body. Paradise is a reality, but only *as a possibility,* which means that the paradise of the spiritual composite of body and soul remains hidden within human nature.[59] Potentially wise, man chose ignorance and the distortion of the divine image. In turn, he dragged down all of creation made in him.

The Abuse of Free Will

The primary cause of the fall is man's misuse of his free will. Sin occurs when man distorts his freedom by choosing to indulge in goods purely in reference to himself, as if they existed apart from God. The cause of evil is "an irrational motion," "the abuse of natural goods, prohibited by divine laws, which is the property of a perverted and illicit desire of each free will that uses the good for evil."[60] Man sought to enjoy creation apart from God, as if it were an autonomous cosmos for his pleasure, and thereby freely cast himself down.

God "knew" of man's transgression from the beginning and allowed man to make his choice and to suffer the consequences.[61] God permitted this fall, in part, as a demonstration of his justice:[62] "Now truly he predestined a mingling not only of beautiful and honest things, but also of dishonest and corrupt things in his creation in order that he might find among these things occasions for the manifestation of his justice. He will give rewards for those living well and honestly according to divine laws, and punishments to transgressors and to those contaminated by the stains of turpitude and dishonesty."[63] In the end, even the brokenness of creation will reveal God's glory through the exercise of judgment in the return.

Yet God primarily allowed the fall in order that man might freely return to his original state and submit to God's will for the union of creation in himself. The experience of creation's devastation and fragmentation

---

59. *Peri.* V, 215, 6971–76.

60. *Peri.* V, 160–61, 5231–35. Also see Augustinus, *De libero arbitrio* III, i, *i–iii*, 274, 1–37.

61. *Prae.* II, iv, 15, 118–25.

62. Original sin inspires the anger of God and the consequent punishments that man receives. "'Fuistis aliquando filii irae sicut et caeteri. (Eph 2:3)' Ira dei potest originale peccatum intelligi, quoniam illud originale peccatum iram dei in humanam naturam provocavit; quod originale peccatum manet in his qui nolunt credere in eum qui pro illis mortuus est." *Comm.* III, xii, 276, 63–66.

63. *Peri.* V, 152, 4932–39.

inspires man to engage in ascetic activity and spiritual purification through the awakened desire to know God. In the fall, God wished that human nature, "purified by action and knowledge and exercised in the studies of wisdom, might recognize itself, and might wish and be able to return to its original happiness, which it had abandoned by sinning."[64] Post-lapsarian creation, therefore, retains its essential dignity and hope within man, who continues to have the potential of divine union in his nature.[65]

The General Consequences of the Fall

The consequences of the fall shape man's mode of existence. First, man loses the spiritual state of his pristine composite nature. His body becomes material flesh as he lives an irrational and unstable existence. The more he submits to this flesh and sensory experience, the more he comes to resemble the beasts.[66] His freedom in this state remains impaired, "impeded by the darkness of Original Sin"[67] and enslaved to irrational impulses.

The greatest tragedy for man, however, is the ignorance that blinds him to the truth and besmears the beauty of creation. Man, in turning toward lesser goods and sensory experience, no longer sees the essences in their divine unity, but rather he perceives them in their scattered manifestations, as if they existed "apart" from God. Man's ignorance of his nature[68] as the divine image naturally leads to a vision of creation in its diversity, a complex of particulars ripe for man's pleasure and exploitation. The turn from God, therefore, leads to the disorder of the fallen cosmos in which the

---

64. *Peri.* V, 8, 162–64. Also see *Peri.* I, 22, 440–51.

65. The hope of creation is sustained in the continuing human capacity to effect the return through its being, willing, and knowing. See *Prae.* IV, vi, 31, 166–69. The first sin was one of will, not of nature, and, therefore, did not impair entirely the potential of man's pristine state. See *Peri.* V, 159, 5170–76.

66. *Comm.* VI, ii, 334–36, 58–61.

67. *Prae.* IV, viii, 34, 231–33.

68. *Peri.* IV, 53, 1442–43. Eriugena teaches that man can never know his essence in itself, just as God cannot "know" or "define" the divine essence. In the end, man can only know "that he is," not "what he is." The ignorance of self that occurs during the fall applies to the loss of the unifying vision of creation in man, a movement from the unity of knowing-being in the human intellect to the divisions of false appearances. See *Peri.* I, 5, 53–64.

breakdown of the hierarchy of man's nature—intellect, vital motion, and body—causes the corruption of all things united in him.[69]

Fallen man, by knowing essences through the obscurity of the senses, weighs down their being with corrupt matter and subjects them to the vicissitudes of decay and mutation: he obscures the intelligible light of creation with the cloud of the mutable senses.[70] His irrationality is the source of "all species, every difference and property of irrationality itself, and all things which are naturally known around it."[71] The one who should have been the locus of deification, becomes the cause of devastation.[72] Yet hope still remains even in this tragic state: "For although the human mind was distanced from its Creator through corruption, nevertheless God never abandoned it for the sake of the dignity of its nature."[73]

The Material Body

In his fallen state man finds himself laboring under the weight of a material body, the flesh. The fallen body must struggle with super-added characteristics (*superadiecta*) that do not belong to the essence of the human body, but emerge as a consequence of sin. These include: "the animal, terrestrial, corruptible body; the sexual distinctions of masculine and feminine; the multiplication through procreation that is similar to [the manner of] beasts; the need for food and drink; the increase and decrease of the body; the alternating and inevitable necessity of sleeping and waking; and other

69. "The mind receives the cause of its formation from God, without the intervention of any creature; the vital motion receives its cause from the mind; and matter receives the cause of its formation from the mind through the vital motion. Thus matter follows vital motion, vital motion follows mind, and, finally, mind follows God. When, therefore, it turns towards Him, it preserves the beauty and integrity of its nature; but when it turns away from Him, it dissipates and disfigures not only itself, but also that which is subject to it—material life and matter itself." *Peri.* IV, 71, 2025–29. Human sin "ultimately frustrates and counteracts the dialectical course of Eriugena's all-embracing *natura*, of which God and creation form the constituent parts but which yet hinges on the development of human nature." Otten, "Role of Man," 604.

70. *Hom.* XII, 260, 4–11.

71. *Peri.* IV, 41, 1104–7.

72. "Consequently, sin forms a direct danger for the evolution of 'natura', for by disturbing man's mediating position, it threatens to hamper the flexible transition from procession to return. More specifically this means that it becomes impossible for man to fulfill his specific task of leading creation back to God." Otten, "Interplay," 12.

73. *Expo.* IV, iii, 75, 410–13.

similar things from all of which human nature, if it had not sinned, would have remained entirely free, and one day will be free."[74] The super-added features stain the purity of the human body and render man's life a time of suffering and confusion.

Eriugena defines this material body as "a certain composition of the four elements compressed together under a certain species. For by this general definition all bodies that consist of matter and form are included under a single description."[75] Two important general features of man's carnal existence emerge from this definition that encompass all of the post-lapsarian additions, the *superadiecta*: the instability of a composite existence and the inauthenticity of material expression.

The Instability and Complexity of Fleshly Existence

A material body consists in the traditional Aristotelian polarity of matter and form. In general, this indicates that fallen man is not simple, but complex. Such bodies are inherently corruptible, since, as composites, they consist in both an enduring form—the essence of the body—and unstable matter.[76] Matter renders a body mortal: a body must one day decay and return to the four elements in which it consists.[77] While man will live forever in his authentic simplicity, the "lowest and most worthless" part of man, the material accretions of the body, will dissolve into the dust of their origins.[78]

The instability of this carnal state reveals that man does not belong to this mode of existence. He is no longer a simple, unified, and spiritual essence, but a fragmented creature in exile.[79] One need only observe the calamities of daily life to understand that something has gone horribly wrong for humanity. Eriugena offers another list of characteristics that now mar the life of the highest of creatures:

---

74. *Peri.* IV, 94, 2801–7. On the manner in which Eriugena attempted to harmonize Augustine and Gregory of Nyssa on this point see d'Onofrio, "Disagreement," 123.

75. *Peri.* I, 47, 1380–84. This definition is contrasted with spirit: "Spirit is an incorporeal nature without form or matter. Every spirit is either rational or intellectual, and it is without form in itself." *Peri.* I, 47, 1384–85.

76. *Peri.* I, 66, 2025–27. Also see *Comm.* III, ii, 210, 30–34.

77. *Peri.* III, 119, 3438–40.

78. *Peri.* IV, 166–67, 5143–51. Also see *Peri.* V, 23, 659–64.

79. *Peri.* I, 68, 2076–77.

> By this [vital motion] the soul administers those things which were superadded to human nature after sin, that is, this corruptible and mortal body, which is variable in motions and times, divided by the number of its parts, stretched out in space, divided by increases and decreases, subjected to different qualities and quantities, and prone to all irrational motions. This body is the guesthouse to a soul that is still carnal because of its disobedience and pride, overwhelmed by various tragedies. And there are other things that are spoken of and known by experience about the unhappiness of human nature, which was expelled from the happiness of paradise into this life.[80]

This negative assessment focuses upon both the moral and physical complexity of post-lapsarian humanity. Morally, pride and disobedience stand out as those sins that render even the soul carnal and imprison the human body within divisible material constraints. Physically, the body remains unstable not only in its corruptibility, but also in its temporal and spatial limitations. In general, man finds himself absorbed by suffering and change because of the loss of simplicity: physically he is torn asunder by unnatural divisions, morally he is divided by false allegiances and misdirected desires. Man now lives in thrall to a deceptive variety of attractions and constraints.[81]

Another result of this loss of simplicity is the division of humanity into male and female. Eriugena, adopting a position of Gregory of Nyssa and Maximus the Confessor,[82] taught that sexual differences belong to this fallen existence: "For if the first man had not sinned, he would not have suffered the partition of his nature into two sexes."[83] Male and female, then, do not define authentic humanity, but rather apply to the fallen body alone. God allowed this to take place as both a means of procreation and punishment for man's transgression: "Indeed, the division of nature into two sexes—I mean male and female—and the generation from them for the continuation and multiplication of humanity because of its decay, are the punishments for general sin, by which all of humanity at once transgressed

---

80. *Peri.* II, 62, 1427–36.

81. Both men and demons lost the simplicity of their original existence, each nature taking on material and aerial bodies. See *Peri.* IV, 157, 4826–34.

82. See Gregorius Nyssenus, *De hominis opificio* XVI, 181A–185D; Maximus, *Ambigua* XLI, 1309A. Also see Thunberg, *Microcosm*, 377.

83. *Peri.* II, 12, 225–27.

God's commandment in paradise."[84] Male and female remain categories in the fallen world for humanity shattered by sin.

The Inauthenticity of Carnal Expression

Eriugena maintains a "bundle theory" of matter in which a material body consists of a conglomeration of spiritual qualities, or accidents, adhering to an essence.[85] Thus material bodies become "real" when an essence is rendered visible through the adjoined immaterial qualities.[86] The fleshly body represents a state in which the spiritual becomes weighted, unstable, and visible, since man separates these spiritual qualities from their authentic unity in God and subjects them to his own selfish will.[87] Yet it must be noted that, while the fallen state of matter—an aggregate of qualities exploited apart from God—is an evil, matter itself is a good in the authentic spiritual state to which it will return in the resurrection.

The inauthenticity of this corrupt material expression becomes evident within Eriugena's discussion of the image and likeness of God in man.

84. *Comm.* I, xxxi, 174, 51–56. Also see *Peri.* IV, 82, 2401–13; Gregorius Nyssenus, *De hominis opificio* XXIV, 212D–213C.

85. Only essences truly exist. Material bodies, since they consist of immaterial accidents, dissolve when those accidents are withdrawn and return to their immaterial state. See *Peri.* I, 84–85, 2612–14. Eriugena attributes his bundle theory primarily to Gregory of Nyssa. See *Peri.* I, 83, 2564–66; Gregorius Nyssenus, *Hexaemeron*, 69B–C; *Anima*, 124B–D. On ancient bundle theories of matter see Blowers, *Drama*, 180–81; Sorabji, *Matter*, 44–59.

86. *Peri.* I, 72, 2206–10.

87. Eriugena's bundle theory may in part find its motivation in Gregory of Nyssa, who sought to explain how matter emerged from spirit: how could the coarseness of the material world come from God? The solution lies in the fact that material bodies, in fact, come from *immaterial* qualities that come together in unique combinations. God creates spirit, while material bodies find their origin in the new, fallen mode of existence as an aggregate of accidents: "How can quantity come from non-quantity, the visible from the invisible, something with limited bulk and size from what lacks magnitude and limits?" Gregorius Nyssenus, *Hexaemeron*, 69B. For commentary on this passage see Sorabji, *Matter*, 52–54.

Yet Eriugena primarily adopts this theory in order to explain how the authentic spiritual composite of man in paradise—the soul and the spiritual body—could descend to the instability of matter. Fallen man, as explained below, becomes visible and unstable by expressing himself through a self-created body that consists of immaterial accidents. Thus the post-lapsarian body becomes the visible expression of man's original soul and spiritual body, and it allows him to live in the fallen world of the effects. See *Peri.* II, 74, 1723–25.

On the one hand, he teaches that the divine image belongs to man's soul, not to the body: "We must understand man to be made in the image of God in his soul alone and in the virtues established in it."[88] On the other hand, the soul—containing the Trinitarian image of power, essence, and energy—impresses the divine image upon the spiritual body.[89] The original soul-body composite as a whole, therefore, reflects the image of God: the soul is the divine image in and of itself, the spiritual body is the divine image in its conformity to the soul.

The weighted material body, as a created state of the pre-lapsarian spiritual composite, expresses the divine image only in a limited way.[90] After the fall, man formed a material body from creation, "a mortal dwelling from the mud of the earth."[91] In effect, God's image—the soul-spiritual body composite—creates its own image, the material body: "God creates the soul out of nothing in his own image, but the soul itself creates its own body, not out of nothing, but out of something."[92] Therefore, the spiritual composite reveals itself through the creation and "careful discipline" of the flesh.[93] Yet man's material body always remains an "image of an image"— the inauthentic and unstable expression of the soul.[94]

In the end, however, this material body cannot endure. Eriugena comes to this logical conclusion based on the principle that anything visible or sensible cannot last.[95] Only spirit, in its simplicity and freedom from confining qualities, lives for eternity. Material expression of the spiritual, as an image twice removed, both reveals and conceals: it can never be the authentic expression of man and it is doomed to pass away.

88. These inherent virtues include wisdom, knowledge, and the power of reason. See *Peri.* IV, 81, 2385–90.

89. *Peri.* II, 56, 1287–1300. Also see *Peri.* II, 57–58, 1319–44.

90. Though Eriugena generally speaks of the soul as the creator of the material body, it is clear that the spiritual body itself—the spiritual expression of the soul—is also a cause. A spiritual body is capable of being the cause of effects below itself, contributing to the formation of immaterial elements that become man's fleshly body. See *Peri.* II, 111–12, 2733–53.

91. *Peri.* II, 79, 1846–49. Also see *Peri.* II, 74, 1725–32.

92. *Peri.* II, 74, 1723–25.

93. *Peri.* II, 75, 1765–66. The inner trinity of the soul—the *authentic* divine image— "cares for the entirety of its body and the safety of its senses; the [inner trinity] gives it life, moves it, and contains it, as much as the fragility of its mortality allows." *Peri.* II, 76, 1783–86.

94. Compare with Plotinus, *Enneades* VI, iii, *xv*, 225.

95. *Comm.* VI, vi, 366, 94–96.

The Status of the Flesh

In the end, what is man's relationship with the material body? Eriugena makes an important distinction near the end of Book One of the *Periphyseon* between "what man is" and "what man has."

> We are our substance (*substantia*),[96] which is life giving and intelligible, beyond the body and all its senses and visible form. What we have—and is not we ourselves—is the body that adheres to us, composed of quantity, quality, and other accidents. It is sensible, mutable, dissoluble, and corruptible. One could say nothing truer than that it is the instrument and seat of the senses, which the Greeks call αἰσθητήρια (that is αἰσθήσεων τήρια, the "guardians of the senses"). Since the soul is incorporeal and cannot reveal its thoughts through itself without the senses; and the senses themselves cannot be guarded except in certain seats, the Founder of Nature established the body for use of the soul, in which it guards its vehicles, that is, the senses.[97]

On the one hand, Eriugena emphasizes that man is not his material body, but rather man finds his identity in his essence (*substantia*). The material body cannot offer a consistent reference point for human nature, since it is constantly in flux. It belongs to man as a divinely intended instrument for interacting with creation and, as we shall see, for realizing the return to divine unity. Yet it must never define what man is. Only the essence, "beyond the body and the senses," establishes man's true identity.

---

96. Though Eriugena is not always consistent in his use of terms, a brief overview of key definitions is in order. "Nature" (*natura*) is a term that embraces all things, "those that are and those that are not," that is, those things that are limited and comprehensible (the effects) and those things which transcend all limiting definition (God, the primordial causes). See *Peri.* I, 3, 9–10. The "primordial causes" (*causae primordiales*) are, in the words of Deirdre Carabine, "the ideas or predestinations of all things in the mind of God made in the Word. . . . The primordial causes are the species or forms in which the reasons [*rationes*] are created before the things themselves come to exist." Carabine, *Eriugena*, 53. All essences and effects participate in the primordial causes, while the causes themselves remain undiminished and distinct from their participants. "Substance" or "essence" (*substantia, essentia, ratio,* οὐσία) represent the totality of distinguishing or defining properties of individuals, though *what* an essence is in itself, that is, what it is in the primordial causes in God, surpasses any definition or comprehensible limitations. See *Peri.* I, 68, 2083–96. "Person" (*persona, substantia,* ὑπόστασις, πρόσωπον) does not indicate the free, self-constituting subject of many modern schools, but rather it simply designates a distinct individual. The term becomes important when discussing the Trinitarian persons or the single person of Christ in two natures.

97. *Peri.* I, 77, 2369–80.

On the other hand, one must not fall into an unhealthy dualism that understands the material body to be a prison. God established the material body in order that man might act in creation and return to his exalted state. In the above passage, Eriugena highlights the body as the seat of the senses and the means by which the soul expresses itself in the fallen world.[98] Man may "possess" his material body—its inconsistency cannot sustain human identity—but this does not mean that it is superfluous or evil. As Eriugena often declares, it is part of God's plan to restore all things:

> For it must not be believed that the Creator's most divine clemency had thrust sinful man into this world as if the Creator were moved by some kind of indignation or was desirous of vengeance—for true reason shows that the divine goodness lacks these qualities—but it occurred as a certain way of ineffable teaching and incomprehensible mercy. God desired that man, who by his free will did not want to preserve himself in the dignity of his nature, might seek the grace of his Creator after learning through his punishments and, through grace, might obey the divine precepts, which he had previously neglected through pride. Thus man, now cautious and prudent, may return to his original state, from whence he, guarded by grace and his free will, might not fall, nor want to fall, nor be able to fall.[99]

Eriugena's reflections upon the material body in fallen man lead to two important conclusions. First, though man should not identify himself with the instability of his material existence, he nonetheless needs his carnal body in order to express his spiritual nature. The body is his own creation, formed and sustained by the soul, and, therefore, images him. Just as the soul reflects the divine image without being God, so also the material body reflects the divine image of the soul without being the soul. The material body does not define a man, but man certainly defines his material body by subjecting it to the virtues of the spirit.

Second, the material body remains the locus of man's return to God. On the one hand, its precarious form of existence, always on the verge of

98. In fact, the material senses reflect the spiritual senses that man shared with the angels. In his disobedience man turned from God and God allowed man to suffer the privation of the spiritual senses in exchange for the carnal senses. See *Expo.* XV, iii, 197, 375–78. The soul requires the body and the senses to manifest its invisible movement. See *Peri.* II, 74, 1725–32. On the positive and negative notions of the senses in Eriugena see Wohlman, "L'homme," 264–65. On the notion of interior or spiritual senses and the fall into carnal senses see Stock, "Philosophical Anthropology," 30–32.

99. *Peri.* II, 22, 440–51.

dissolution, acts as a goad to awaken man to his true nature. God allows fallen man to form a material body for himself in order that man might experience the sufferings and longings of material existence. The instability and loss of simplicity that man endures daily inspire him to look beyond the variety of sensory experience toward God and his authentic self. On the other hand, man acts through the body in order to grow in virtue and direct himself toward the unity of God. Without the material body, man could not participate in the reformation of creation in Christ.

Preserving Man in the Incarnate Word

An important problem emerges from Eriugena's understanding of man's creation and fall. God freely and lovingly manifested himself in the creation of man, the primary knower and locus of creation. Yet if man never actually existed in this paradisiacal state, how are the effects known in man's intellect—including the concept of his own nature[100]—preserved from annihilation? In other words, if the knower and conveyer of being has fallen, what—or who—stabilizes the being of the fallen order?

As we have already seen, Eriugena finds his solution by grounding authentic humanity—and, in turn, all of creation—in the Word. In paradise the definition of man is "a rational substance (*substantia*) capable of wisdom."[101] Yet the *real* definition of man is "a certain intellectual concept eternally made in the mind of God."[102] Therefore, man is most truly himself in God, that is, in the eternal divine conception of man in the Word. This unique essence of man remains immutable in God, even after man's betrayal of his mission.[103]

This establishment of man in the Word may be taken one step further: Eriugena suggests that man is preserved in the *incarnate* Word. The Incarnation—the Word's decent into man's fallen, material state—should not be understood simply as a temporal event. In fact, it is an eternal reality, the divine intention that preserves, restores, and elevates all things: "He

100. "That concept by which man knows himself is his own substance." *Peri.* IV, 43, 1149–50.

101. *Prae.* VIII, iv, 50, 72–74.

102. *Peri.* IV, 40, 1072–73.

103. Man has "one substance conceived in two ways": one in its true condition in the intellect, the other in the effects. See *Peri.* IV, 44, 1178–81. Regarding the body in the eternal definition of man see Steel, "Return," 603.

does not cease to shine, nor does he want to desert [human nature], despite its fault, nor did he ever desert it. He formed it by containing it through nature, and reformed it by deifying it through grace."[104]

The divine intention to sustain and restore creation through the Incarnation effectively *is* the Word's assumption of human nature from all eternity. Thus Eriugena interprets the "All-Tree" of paradise (Gen 2:9)—"before" the fall of man even takes place—as the incarnate Word, who is the archetype, exemplar, and sustainer of human nature and creation:

> And the πᾶν ξύλον (that is, "the All-Tree") is the Word and Wisdom of the Father, our Lord Jesus Christ, who is every fruit-bearing tree, planted in the midst of human nature in two ways. First, according to his divinity, by which he creates, contains, nourishes, vivifies, illuminates, deifies, moves, and causes our nature to be: "In Him we live, and move, and have our being" (Acts 17:28). Second, according to our nature, which he joined to himself in order that he might subsist in two natures, divine and human, and might save human nature and recall it to its pristine state. And this is what Scripture says: "The Lord, God, produced the All-Tree from the earth" (Gen 2:9), that is, from our material nature. The All-Tree is the incarnate Word, in whom and through whom all things are made, and who is all things.[105]

God preserves creation through the eternal desire to descend and be one with man in his brokenness. One cannot, therefore, distinguish between what the Word does according to his divinity (creating, nourishing, vivifying, etc.) and what the Word does according to our nature (sustaining, restoring and elevating) since he is incarnate in the eternal intention of God. The All-Tree—the incarnate Word—enfolds creation from the beginning as the foundation and hope of humanity.

Conclusions

This chapter examined Eriugena's notions of human embodiment and the significance of the flesh. Man is a composite being, consisting of body and

104. *Comm.* I, xxv, 116–18, 22–26. A lengthy addition from *i²* includes an important interpretation that places the essences of all things eternally in Christ's humanity: "For all intelligible essences, which Christ assumed, inseparably adhere to his *human intellect.*" *Peri.* II, 24, 255–57. On the eternal conjoining of Christ's divinity and humanity see Moran, "Idealism," 76.

105. *Peri.* IV, 116, 3482–92.

soul. He has only one body, but that body may be considered in two states. First, there is the authentic spiritual state of the body in paradise, that is, pristine human nature, which remains hidden within man. Second, there is the material state after the fall, marred by the scars of sin. Man's body is one, but it now must be liberated from the constraints of fallen existence.

Man's composite nature is essential for the fulfillment of his vocation, since it renders him "the workshop of the world," who unites all things in himself: when man understands himself and all things formed in him, he bestows being on them through his knowing. When man refused, however, to see things in divine unity, choosing the exploitative vision of fragmented variety, he dragged himself and all of creation down to the mutable and distorted state of material existence. The restoration and deification of all things, therefore, depends upon the salvation of composite man and the recovery of his authentic vision of creation.

For Eriugena, the term *incarnatio* refers specifically to the eternally willed descent of the Word into the fallen effects, that is, into the fleshly state of man. The Word, in becoming flesh, takes on all the *superadiecta* of this state, with the exception of sin itself, in order to restore and elevate all of creation. Furthermore, he assumes the full history of man's body in the drama of the fall and redemption: from the spiritual body of paradise hidden within man's nature, to the broken body that becomes man's material expression. The following chapters explore the full import and meaning of this enfleshment of the Word.

2

Jesus Christ

God and Man

THIS CHAPTER EXAMINES ERIUGENA'S UNDERSTANDING of the metaphysical underpinnings of the Incarnation (*incarnatio* or *inhumanatio*) of the Word. It begins by considering the limited scope of the term "Incarnation," as compared to other forms of divine condescension.[1] Next, it summarizes his appropriation of the riches of the Christian theological tradition and concludes with an overview of Eriugena's teachings regarding the two natures of Christ and the hypostatic union.

The Term "Incarnation"

Incarnation and "Quasi-Incarnation"

Generally Eriugena limits the term "Incarnation" to Jesus: the Incarnation is the descent of the Word into fallen creation, that is, into the effects fragmented by man's sin and ignorance. The Word humbles himself by being born of the Virgin and assuming the limitations of the flesh.

---

1. *Condescensio* or συγκατάβασις are traditional terms for the Incarnation, indicating God's descent to be "with" fallen humanity and creation.

Yet adapting a teaching from Maximus the Confessor,[2] Eriugena describes three modes in which the Word condescends and ascends in creation:

> Indeed, the garment of the Word is visible creation, which preaches him openly and manifests his beauty to us. The Holy Scriptures have also been made his garment, which contain the mysteries. . . . There are the two feet of the Word, one of which is the natural reason of visible creation and the second of which is the spiritual understanding of the Sacred Scriptures. The sensible forms of the sensible world cover the former, while the surface of the divine letters, that is, of the Scriptures, cover the latter. Thus the instructors of the divine law teach the Incarnation of the Divine Word in two modes (*duobus modis*). One of them teaches his Incarnation from the Virgin, by which he joined human nature to himself in a unity of substance (*substantia*) (1). The other teaches that the Word is quasi-incarnate (*quasi incarnatum*), that is, rendered thick (*incrassatum*) by the letters (2), as well as by the forms and orders of visible things (3).[3]

One can, in fact, distinguish three modes of divine condescension in this passage: condescension in the Scriptures, in creation, and in the birth from the Virgin. Eriugena does not, however, understand the modes to be equal and he clearly qualifies Maximus's teaching. He admits that the Word becomes "visible," "intelligible," and even "corporeal" through creation (mode 3) and the Scriptures (mode 2), which are accessible to the senses, reason, and spiritual intelligence.[4] These two modes, however, are qualified when compared with the Incarnation from the Virgin (mode 1): the Word is "quasi-incarnate" in creation and the Scriptures, and therefore *truly* incarnate only as Jesus Christ. The term "Incarnation" applies primarily to

---

2. See Eriugena, *Ambigua* XXXIII (29), 166–67, 1–24; Maximus, *Ambigua* XXXIII, 1285C–D. For the source of this commentary see Gregorius Nazianzenus, *Oratio* XXXVIII, ii, 106, 16–21. Thomas Böhm also highlights Eriugena's appropriation of the Maximian theme of mediation through the incarnate Word. See Böhm, "Adnotationes," 51–53. As we shall see, however, Eriugena embraces, in part, the Maximian teaching that the Incarnation extends beyond the historical person of Jesus into all of deified creation: the multivalence of God "rendered thick."

3. *Comm.* I, xxix, 154–56, 52–68. Also see *Peri.* V, 203, 6578–81; *Hom.* XI, 254, 11–18.

4. On this theme see Duclow, "Dialectic," 109.

the descent of the Word into the effects, secondarily to the Scriptures and "visible things."[5]

Theosis, or deification, is the truest theophany of the Word in creation (mode three for Eriugena). Like Maximus, Eriugena believes that deification represents a form of Incarnation, though he avoids applying the term *incarnatio* to this elevation of man to divinity. The *Nutritor*, in Book One of the *Periphyseon*, summarizes Maximus's doctrine:[6]

> Maximus said that theophany takes place in no other way except through God, truly from the condescension of the divine Word, that is, from the only-begotten Son, who is the Wisdom of the Father. He came down to human nature that had been created and cleansed by himself and then raised it up to the previously mentioned Word through divine love. I am not speaking of the condescension that already took place through the Incarnation, but that condescension which takes place through *theosis* (that is, through deification) of the creature. Theophany, therefore, takes place through the condescension itself of the Wisdom of God to human nature through grace and through the exaltation of the same nature to Wisdom itself through love. In this sense, the holy father Augustine seems to agree when explaining the Apostle's teaching: "Who was made Justice and Wisdom for us" (1 Cor

5. The various "incarnations" of the Word may be understood under the categories of divine omnipresence and theophany: "Thus it [theophany] can apply equally to the descent of Christ into the primordial causes at the creation of the world, to his condescension upon the souls of the blessed during their earthly life when they experience 'ecstasy' (*excessus mentis*), to Christ's actual coming in the flesh and his historical life on earth, and to his descent into the minds of the faithful at the Last Judgment. . . . From God's viewpoint, the various theophanies are one and the same—there is only one *Logos*—but from man's point of view, which is necessarily encumbered by the spatio-temporality of the created world, they are different—the *Logos* is multiplied into a number of *logoi* by the creature." Gersh, "Omnipresence," 68–69.

6. Jeauneau suggests that Eriugena is drawing upon three of the *Ambigua* here: 1) Eriugena, *Ambigua* VII (18), 31, 305–9; Maximus, *Ambigua* VII, 1084B–C. Here, Maximus discusses the deification of man through the conformity to the preexistent *logoi* in the *Logos* and through grace. The result is a form of divine Incarnation: "God becomes man, because of the divinization of man, and man becomes God, because of the humanization of God. In fact the *Logos* of God and God desire that mystery of his Incarnation take place always and in all." 2) Eriugena, *Ambigua* X (6), 48–49, 140–45; Maximus, *Ambigua* X, 1113A–B. Here, Maximus uses his famous expression that God and man are "paradigms of one another": God becomes man and man becomes God through man's conformity to the *logoi* and grace. 3) Eriugena, *Ambigua* LX (56), 237, 22–31; Maximus, *Ambigua* LX, 1385B–C. Maximus discusses the union of man with God in relation to the Incarnation and ascension of the *Logos*.

1:30). He explains as follows: "The Wisdom of the Father, in which and through which all things were made, which is not created, but creates, is made in our souls by a certain ineffable condescension of his mercy and he joins our intellect to himself in order that, in an ineffable way, a certain quasi-composite wisdom comes about from his very condescension to us and his living in us, and from our intellect that he assumes to himself through love and forms in himself."[7]

The passage above distinguishes two modes of the Word's condescension and ascension—two modes that are so close that Eriugena must pause to delineate them for his reader. The first is the Incarnation that "had already taken place," that is, the birth of Jesus, God-made-man, and his return to the Father (mode 1). This condescension and ascension bring about, as we shall see, the restoration and elevation of man (the nature "created and cleansed by himself"). This is the Incarnation in its truest sense.

The other mode of the Word's condescension and ascension, however, takes place through the synergy between human and divine natures by action (ascetical practice) and grace (divine gift): *theosis*, or deification (mode 3), in which man becomes one with God. Eriugena states that the Word "came down to human nature that had been created and cleansed by himself and then raised it up to the previously mentioned Word through divine love." In other words, *after* the Incarnation that is the birth from the Virgin—the condescension and ascension that cleansed human nature—there takes place a second condescension and ascension through the elevation of man to the divine. This movement of *theosis* is so close to that of the Incarnation that Eriugena stops to distinguish them clearly: "I say that this condescension is *not* that which already took place through the Incarnation, but that which takes place through *theosis* (that is, through deification) of the creature."

Eriugena's adaptation of Maximus's multivalent understanding of the Word's descent and ascent in creation reveals the limited scope of the term "Incarnation." On the one hand, Eriugena truly shares Maximus's *Logos*-centric vision, in which all of creation comes from the Word and is deified by the Word. This allows him to accept various modes in which the Word "becomes thick" (*incrassatus*). Thus the descent and ascent of the Word in

7. *Peri.* I, 13, 296–317. It is not known where Eriugena obtained this quote from Augustine.

deification is a form of "Incarnation," since the Word becomes enfleshed in deified humanity—the Word is *quasi incarnatum*.

On the other hand, the term "Incarnation" applies primarily to the birth of the Word from the Virgin and his ascension to the Father. This unique event cannot be equated with any other theophany. Eriugena is no pantheist, for whom creation itself—even through the mediation of deified humanity—is equated with God. Though creation will be one with God through the Word, it can never truly *be* God, who remains without cause and within the inscrutable divine darkness. Even deified humanity cannot be called divine in the fullest sense. Jesus Christ alone is God-made-flesh.

Councils, Controversies, and Terminology

Goulven Madec notes that Eriugena does not concern himself with the development of doctrine during the formative centuries of early Christianity, but rather focuses upon the authority of the tradition in transmitting the essential truths.[8] Yet the vocabulary and modes of thought within the tradition certainly contribute to his understanding of Jesus Christ. A brief consideration of his appropriation of the *theologorum traditio* demonstrates this influence.[9]

Versus Docetism

Eriugena demonstrates an awareness of previous christological and Trinitarian controversies and the significance of their hard-won doctrines. For example, he rejects any form of docetism that would render the Incarnation an illusion.[10] The Incarnation must be a genuine enfleshment for the sake of all creation: "[The Word appeared] not through an angel to angels, nor through an angel to men, but through a man to both men and angels. He did not become manifest in a false appearance (*phantasia*), but in true humanity itself, which he assumed to himself in its entirety in a unity of substance [*substantia*, person]. In this way he made himself known to all

8. Madec, "Jean Scot," 150.

9. Eriugena highlights that to which the tradition of the theologians adheres (*theologorum traditio universaliter consentit*), while acknowledging that the Fathers did disagree on some issues. *Peri.* V, 25, 715.

10. On the negative sense of *phantasia* in Eriugena see *Peri.* V, 118, 3797–3812. Also see Foussard, "Apparence et apparition," 339.

intelligent beings."[11] The hypostatic union—union "of substance" in Eriugena's terms[12]—precludes any reduction of the Incarnation to a vision or dream. The Word became human, uniting two natures in his person.[13]

Versus Arianism

Eriugena also attacks the Arians for their demotion of the Divine Word to the level of a creature and for failing to teach the unity of essence in the Godhead with its substantial distinctions, that is, distinctions among the persons of the Father, Son, and Spirit:

> And lest someone think that the Word subsists "in the beginning" in a such a way that no difference of substances [persons] is to be understood, [John the Evangelist] then adds: "And the Word was with God" (John 1:1), that is, "And the Son subsists with the Father in a unity of essence and substantial distinction."
>
> And again, lest such a poisonous contagion should creep into someone that teaches that the Word is only in the Father and with God, but that the Word itself does not subsist substantially [that is, as a distinct person] and coessentially with the Father as God—for this error infected the perfidious Arians—he [the Evangelist] next adds: "And the Word was God (John 1:1)."[14]

In his refutation of the Arians, he once again affirms the traditional distinction between the unity of the divine essence (*essentia*) and the distinctions among persons (*substantia*). In Book Two of the *Periphyseon*, Eriugena, in the voice of the *Alumnus*, expresses his great respect for the Fathers—especially Dionysius, Gregory of Nazianzus, and Maximus—and their teachings regarding the Trinity.[15] When speaking of the Trinity one says that "there is a difference between οὐσία, that is, essence (*essentia*), and ὑπόστασις, that is, substance (*substantia*). Indeed they [the Fathers] understand οὐσία to be the unique and simple nature of divine goodness,

11. *Hom.* III, x, 256–58, 31–36.

12. Eriugena preferred a literal translation of the term *hypostasis* as *substantia*. See *Peri.* V, 221–22, 7186–96; *Hom.*, 259, n. 2.

13. Eduard Jeauneau credits the influence of the Chalcedonean Christology of Maximus the Confessor for the "realism" of Eriugena's Christology: "Ce réalisme fait contrepoids, en quelque sorte, aux tendances néoplatoniciennes, si fortes dans la pensée érigiénne." Jeauneau, "Jean l'Érigène," 204.

14. *Hom.* VI, 228, 15–24.

15. See *Peri.* II, 120, 3025–27. Also see *Peri.* I, 23, 596–99.

but the ὑπόστασις is the property of the individual persons and individual substances. They say μίαν οὐσίαν ἐν τρισίν ὑποστάσεσιν, that is, one essence in three substances."[16] In the same passage he also demonstrates knowledge of the Greek term πρόσωπον, translating it as "person" (*persona*) and acknowledging its appropriateness for expressing the distinctions among Father, Son, and Spirit.[17] He concludes by confessing the Trinity in the words of the church fathers: "Therefore the Father subsists through himself, the Son subsists [through himself], the Holy Spirit subsists [through himself]; and three substances subsist in one essence, since the Three are One."[18]

Eriugena asserts that these Trinitarian distinctions are by relation, not by nature. In this way he accepts Gregory of Nazianzus's refutation of Eunomius and obviates the charge of subordinationism.[19] Gregory and the Fathers taught that "the relation (*habitus*) of the unbegotten substance [person] to the begotten substance is the Father; the relation of the begotten substance to the unbegotten substance is the Son; and the relation of the proceeding substance to the unbegotten and begotten substances is the Holy Spirit."[20] Eriugena approves of this understanding of Trinitarian relations because it preserves both the distinctions of persons and the unity of essence.[21]

The substantial relations of the Trinity and the unity of essence come to the fore when Eriugena treats the question of whether the Son is born, and the Spirit proceeds, from the substance [person] of the Father alone,

---

16. *Peri.* II, 120–21, 3025–32. Also see *Hom.* VI, 228, 18–19: "Et filius subsistit cum patre in unitate essentiae et substantiali distinctione."

17. See *Peri.* II, 121, 3039.

18. *Peri.* II, 121, 3050–52.

19. *Peri.* I, 24, 621–28. Also see Gregorius Nazianzenus, *Orationes* XXIX, xvi, 210–12.

20. *Peri.* I, 24, 606–10. For sources see Gregorius Nazianzenus, *Orationes* XXIX, xvi, 210–12; Maximus, *Ambigua* XXII, 1265C–1268B. Of course, Maximus has adapted the formulation of the Spirit's role in order to accommodate the *filioque*. Elsewhere, Eriugena will express these relations as primary substantial cause or origin (Father) and secondary substantial causes (Son, Spirit): the relations are entirely logical, causal distinctions and do not imply divisions by nature. "In causa itaque omnium est causa praecedens et sunt causae sequentes. . . . Maior quippe pater est filio non secundum naturam sed secundum causam. Pater namque causa est filii, non autem filius causa est patris." *Peri.* II, 102–3, 2481–82; 2488–91.

21. The Eunomians, in asserting that the names indicated essences or natures, taught subordination within the Trinity and denied the full divinity of the Son and Spirit. See *Peri.* I, 25, 632–34.

or from the divine essence. In his response, Eriugena, in the voice of the *Nutritor*, claims to maintain the "teaching of the Catholic Faith":

> If, therefore, the divine essence, because it is one and the same, is neither the Father nor the Son nor the Holy Spirit, but is the common nature of them all, it follows that the Son is not begotten of the essence, nor does the Holy Spirit proceed from it. For if the Son is begotten of the essence, he is not begotten of the Father, for the essence itself, as we said, is not the Father. In a similar way, if the Holy Spirit proceeds from the same essence, he does not proceed from the Father. If, however, the Catholic Faith very firmly and very wisely believes and teaches that the Son is begotten of the Father and the Holy Spirit proceeds from the same Father, does it not follow that we believe and understand that the Son is begotten of the substance [person] of the Father and the Holy Spirit proceeds from him? Thus the Son is begotten, and the Holy Spirit proceeds, not from the essence, but from the substance [person] of the Father.[22]

The Nicene-Constantinopolitan Creed, inclusive of the *filioque,* serves as the touchstone for Eriugena's Trinitarian doctrine and he draws from this tradition in the formulation of his Christology. The distinctions and unity of the persons, the preexistence of the Son, the affirmation of the Son's birth in history—all these positions emerge from Eriugena's affirmation of this Creed, which he places alongside the Scriptures as being "preserved from all heresy."[23]

Eriugena, therefore, demonstrates an awareness of the Greek terminology used in the Trinitarian controversies, the problems of translating these terms into Latin (e.g., *substantia* or *persona* for *hypostasis*),[24] and the

22. *Peri.* II, 122, 3065–76.

23. "In the ineffable and supernatural fecundity of divine Goodness, where from the heart (that is, from hidden interior) of God the Father, the Son is born and the Holy Spirit proceeds, the Catholic Faith requires us to confess that this same Holy Spirit proceeds from the Father and the Son, or from the Father through the Son. But in the Creed of neither language [Greek or Latin], nor in the Scriptures, did I find that the Son is born from the Father through the Spirit. And why is this so? Up until now I have not answered this question myself, nor have I read or found an answer from anyone. When, however, the Scriptures and the Creed that was handed on from the holy synod in Nicea, a city in Bithynia, and preserved from all heresies, are consulted regarding the inhumanization of the Son of God (that is, the Incarnation of the Word), it is clearly evident to us that it is taught without any ambiguity that the Word was conceived by the Holy Spirit." *Peri.* II, 118, 2952–64.

24. See *Peri.* II, 57, 1302–12.

issues regarding the *filioque* in the Western Creed. He understands his own speculations regarding the Trinity and the Incarnation of the Son to be in accord with the Nicene-Costantinopolitan faith, since he affirms the unity of the Godhead and the distinct substances [persons] of Father, Son, and Spirit.

Versus Nestorianism and Monophysitism

Eriugena condemns Nestorianism, which he understands to be the heresy that renders Jesus two persons, a divine and a human. The position was untenable because it effectively taught two Lords, or two Sons. One must, according to the Catholic Faith, affirm only one substance [person] and two natures in Christ.[25]

He also clearly rejects monophysitism, the reduction of Christ to one divine nature. The Creed of Chalcedon, with its strong diphysite language, shapes Eriugena's terminology and approach to the composition of Christ.[26] In his *Expositiones in Ierarchiam Coelestem*, the essential doctrines of the Council regarding the two natures in one person and the *communicatio idiomatum*—the preservation of both the divine and human characteristics in the one person of Christ—contribute to a sound refutation of monophysitism:

> It is clear that the Lord of the celestial powers and the King of Glory, in his humanity, which he accepted from us for our sake, was assumed into heaven, that is, that the humanity of our Lord Jesus Christ, who is Lord of the powers and the King of Glory, was raised up after the resurrection into his divinity, which is called "heaven." The properties of each nature, divine and human, remained without change in the unity of substance [person]: just as

25. "'Lord, Lord, open up to us' (Matt 25:11). This repetition of the name of the Lord, however, means either human nature's continuous desire to contemplate its Creator, when no cloud of ignorance obstructs it, as in the case of those who lived in this life unsupported by the aid of a good conduct; or it certainly signifies the sloth of the simple faithful—those who consider less the loftiness of the Catholic faith—who think that our Lord Jesus Christ was composed of two substances [persons], since he is one substance [person] in two natures. They seek things that are not appropriate for them." *Peri.* V, 221, 7175–85.

26. Eriugena's understanding of the council came especially through the lens of his mentor, Maximus the Confessor. On the significance of Maximus on this point see Jeauneau, "Pseudo-Dionysius," 147–48.

the Word was made flesh, so the flesh was made Word, fully God in the full natures.[27]

Eriugena vehemently defends the hypostatic union, making this doctrine the framework for his discussions on the incarnate Word. "How many are there who divide our Lord Jesus Christ such that they believe or understand neither that his divinity is united with his humanity nor that his humanity is united with his divinity in a unity of substance or, as the Latins say, in a unity of person? For are not his humanity and divinity one and inseparably one, with the distinction of each nature itself preserved?"[28] In Jesus,

> A double essence (*substantia*)[29] produces one person (*persona*): for the eternal God, assuming the principle (*ratio*) [of human nature] in time, after the body was joined, made himself fully man (*perfecerat* ἄνδρα).[30]

When speaking about the hypostatic union, Eriugena does not stand out as an innovator. He does show a preference for a more literal translation of *hypostasis* as "substantia," as opposed to the Latin "persona," but in general he exhibits the principal desire to keep his teachings in continuity with the Fathers and councils.

The Question of Monothelitism

Eriugena does not evince knowledge of the monothelite controversy—the debate over whether Christ possessed both a divine will and a human will—that his mentor, Maximus the Confessor, confronted at the cost of

27. *Expo.* VII, iii, 108–9, 659–68. On this passage see Rorem, *Pseudo-Dionysius*, 158–59.

28. *Peri.* V, 221–22, 7190–96. Regarding the integrity of the two natures of Christ after the resurrection see *Peri.* V, 186, 6069–73: "For he is entirely God, he is whole everywhere, he is wholly exalted over everything which is said and understood, entire in the Father and made one with the Father, full God in full humanity, while the principles of each nature remain themselves in Him."

29. Again, Eriugena is not always consistent with his terms. Here he uses the term *substantia* in the sense of "essence."

30. *Carm.* VIII, 88, 67–68. M. Herren translates *ratio* as "Word," rendering the line, "For God eternal, when he assumed the Word in time." This translation is problematic, since it is the humanity that God assumes in time, not the Word. In this instance, Eriugena is using *ratio* to designate the distinct set of properties of a full human nature. See *Peri.* V, 86, 2736–41; 221–22, 7190–96.

his life.[31] One does not even find, for instance, the Maximian distinction between the so-called deliberative will (γνώμη), which entails free choice and the possibility of error, and the natural will (θέλημα), which chooses the good for the fulfillment of a particular nature.

He does, however, take interest in the free will of humans and angels, making it the essential characteristic of rational and intellectual beings: "Take away the rational will, and there will be no man."[32] He then asks whether freedom belongs to man by nature, or whether it was a super-added divine gift. In fact, he concludes, God must have given man a free will right from the beginning in order that he might freely obey the divine command and, through grace, rise up to a greater union: "Therefore, it must be understood that the first will of man was created naturally free, so that something could be super-added to it later (that is, grace), if he should wish to preserve the Creator's command."[33] Even after the fall, the natural free will remains in man, though it was weakened through the act of disobedience.

The Word, in becoming man, restores the full freedom of the natural human will:

> And human nature is not only will, but also free will. His freedom is not false, but true. Yet liberty itself after sin is so vitiated that it is impeded by its punishment and so does not want to live rightly or, if it should so desire, is not able to live rightly. It is freed from this misery, as the apostle says, by the grace of God through Jesus Christ (Rom 7:25). Its natural liberty remains, as shown by its appetite for happiness, which is implanted in it naturally.[34]

In recognizing that Jesus heals the vitiated human will, Eriugena draws upon Augustine and the Scriptures, and does not make use of the rich anthropological developments that emerged during the monothelite controversy. As we shall see, this does not mean that his Christology fails to take into account human freedom, though Maximus's contributions would most likely have enriched it.

---

31. For instance see Maximus, *Opuscula* XVI, 192B; *Opuscula* VII, 80A.

32. *Prae.* VIII, iii, 50, 45–47.

33. *Prae.* VIII, v, 51, 89–92.

34. *Prae.* V, iv, 37, 94–101.

The Human Nature of Christ

"[Christ] was incarnate in human nature."[35] This means that the Word assumed all of human nature, not simply the mind or soul. "Thus if the Word of God assumed human nature, he did not assume part of it, which is nothing, but its entirety. And if he assumed the whole, he restored the whole perfectly in himself, since all things are restored in him. He abandoned nothing of human nature, which he received in its totality, to be prey to eternal punishments and to the indissoluble web of malice, which the ruin of torments follows."[36] Eriugena expresses the classical principle of patristic Christology: that which the Word did not assume, he did not save.

Assuming the Fullness of Human Nature

Eriugena demonstrates that the Word assumed every part of man. All the components of man belong to Christ as his own: "The Word became flesh, that is, the Word became a whole man, consisting in flesh, soul, and mind."[37] The error associated with Apollinaris, in which the Son substitutes for the human mind in Christ, remains far from the Irishman's thought.[38]

In the poetry, Eriugena highlights the manner in which the Word not only unites the components of human nature to his divinity, but also joins the divisions of creation itself. He uses the distinctions of mind, body, and divinity to demonstrate how Christ heals the fragmented cosmos:

> Christ was incarnate, being born of the Virgin;
> he was nailed to the wood, confined to the tomb;
> Dying in the *body*, living in the *soul* and *divinity*,
> He is God and he dies in order that the *flesh* (*caro*) itself may live.

35. "'In propria ergo venit' (John 1:11), hoc est, in humana natura incarnatus est." *Comm.* I, xx, 94, 1–2.

36. *Peri.* V, 89, 2853–58.

37. *Peri.* IV, 6, 101–3.

38. In an extended addition from the commentator *i²*, one finds a bipartite anthropology—body and soul—associated with related faculties—sense and intellect: "For human nature is constituted by these four parts, which Christ, as true man, assumed and united in himself. Indeed he was made perfect man. For he abandoned no part of man, except for sin, which he did not assume into the unity of his substance and did not unite to himself, that is, he did not make it one. For after the resurrection in him there were not four, but one, and not a composite one, but simply one body and sense, soul and intellect." *Peri.* II, 23, 229–36.

> His *mind* (*mens*) holds Erebus; his *body* (*corpus*), the rock;
> his *divinity* (*numen*), all things
> He is one in three: body (*corpus*), mind (*mens*), and God (*Deus*).[39]

Since Christ assumed the body and spirit/mind of man, the healing of the cosmos extends from the spiritual realm of the dead (Erebus), to the material elements of the fallen world (the rock), to the totality of the causes (all things). He unites and deifies through himself. All things are raised up in him:

> For Christ came down to assume an earthly garment;
> Putting on this garment, he flew upward with it,
> He turned this garment, which he had assumed from the Virgin, into God,
> unifying the soul (*anima*), flesh (*caro*), and divinity (*Deus*).[40]

If the Word is to save man through his descent and ascent, he must assume *all* the parts of man. When the Word says that "I came forth from the Father and came into the world (John 16:28)," he means that "I assumed the form of a servant and the entirety of human nature, that is, body, soul and intellect, and everything in its entirety, which is from creation itself (which consists of visible and intelligible existence)."[41]

Assuming the Flesh

The Incarnation means to become "enfleshed," to take on the broken state of man's fallen existence. In commenting on the verse, "I am a worm and not a man" (Ps 22:6), Eriugena highlights the reality of the flesh that the Word received from the Virgin: "For this [image of the worm] applies to Christ, who is not born of human seed, but, like a worm, is born from the simple nature of the earth. Thus he himself assumed flesh from the flesh of the perpetual and untouched Virgin."[42] Jesus's material body comes from the "earth" of fallen man through the conception in the Virgin's womb.

The Word, in becoming man, takes on not only human nature, but also all those things that were super-added to human nature after the fall,

39. *Carm.* VII, 82, 7–12.
40. *Carm.* IX, 90, 25–28.
41. *Peri.* V, 72, 2300–2304.
42. *Prae.* VIII, 49, 1068–74.

with the exception of sin.[43] Christ was not spirit alone, aloof from the sufferings of humanity, but rather he may rightly be called flesh—the state of fallen existence: "If, however, the whole man, soul as well as body, is reborn in Christ and is made spirit, it is necessary that the whole man in Adam from the flesh be reborn and be flesh. And so one may conclude that flesh may be called spirit, and spirit flesh. The Word of God [in the Scriptures] is called flesh and flesh the Word."[44]

In particular, the Word accepts the mortality of human flesh. The punishment for disobedience becomes part of the Word's existence:

> Thus the flesh of Christ was made mortal for our sake, in order that by his death our death might be entirely destroyed. For the flesh of Christ was not made mortal because of his sin, like our flesh, but it was rendered passible through a condescension to the form of our nature after sin. Though he did not refuse to suffer death for our sake, he did not actually receive the cause of death, that is, sin. Therefore, death was not able to contain him, because he was not a debtor to death. Death could not hold him captive, because it did not find him guilty. Thus Christ received his state of being without sin from the first man, that is, the man who existed before sin; He received the possibility of death from that same man, but from the state of that man after he had sinned. By these two men—the man before sin and the man after sin—he restored our nature in himself.[45]

In this passage, the incarnate Word unites "two men": the man before the fall and the man after the fall.[46] The Incarnation restores unity to

---

43. *Peri.* V, 36, 1103–7.

44. *Peri.* III, 125, 3626–30.

45. *Comm.* I, xxix, 150–52, 24–36.

46. Eriugena develops an idea from Boethius's *Contra Eutychen et Nestorium.* Boethius distinguishes three modes of Adam or humanity: 1) Adam if he had obeyed God. In this mode there would be no death, no sin, nor even the will to sin. 2) Adam before he had made a choice to obey or not obey God. In this mode there was no sin, but the possibility of sinning was present. 3) Adam after disobeying God. In this mode there is sin and the will to sin. The Incarnation assumes elements from these three modes: "For he assumed a mortal body in order that he might drive death away from humanity, because of that state inflicted as a punishment after Adam's crime. What was not in Christ was the will to sin, because he assumed an aspect of the mode that might have been if Adam had not applied his will to the falsehoods of the tempter. There remains therefore the third mode, that of the middle, that which was when death was not present and the will to sin was a possibility. In that time, therefore, Adam was such that he ate and drank, digested the food he received, fell asleep, and all the other human things which were not lacking to

man by eliminating the bifurcation between man's spiritual body (state of the first man) and material body (state of the second man): "For our Lord Jesus Christ, Creator and Savior of human nature, received [the mode of existence] from the first man before sin and the [mode of existence] of the second man after sin. What did he receive from the first man, who was before sin? He acquired the absence of sin, because human nature, before it had sinned, was entirely free of sin. What did he receive from the second man, who was after sin? He acquired death because of sin, while he was still free of the crime of sin."[47] Jesus unites the two modes of human existence in himself, canceling the punishments incurred through the transgressions of the "second man."

Eriugena develops this traditional Adam-Christ typology in two ways. On the one hand, he makes it the basis for Jesus's exaltation over all creation, since he assumed the original state of Adam. Jesus is above all things not only because he is divine, but also because he is truly human: he is God who assumes the paradise of human nature—Adam before the fall. He is the one who preserves authentic humanity in himself: "Thus we must believe that the only-begotten Son of God is above all things in two ways: first, because he is exalted over all humanity, since he came from that very humanity before it had sinned; second, because he is above every creature according to the height of his divinity, in which he is equal to the Father."[48] Creation may therefore adore him because he is truly God and *truly man*.[49]

On the other hand, he makes this typology the basis for Jesus's healing of creation, since Jesus takes on the fallen state of Adam. As we shall see in the next chapter, in becoming mortal, Christ reshapes the mode of man's existence from within. The Word reforms humanity and creation because he enters into solidarity with the second man, the fallen Adam.

---

him as a man, but were allowed and incurred no punishment of death." Boethius, *Contra Eutychen et Nestorium* VIII, 126, 63–76 (LCL translation). The Word therefore assumes death from the third mode; he assumes the freedom from the will to sin from the first mode; and he assumes the simple physical functions of man from the second mode.

47. *Comm.* III, xi, 266, 39–46.

48. *Comm.* III, xi, 266, 55–60.

49. The priority of Jesus comes from both his divinity and authentic humanity: "'Quia prior me erat (John 1:30),' non solum aeternitate divinitatis, sed verum etiam humanitatis dignitate." *Comm.* I, xiv, 108, 35–36.

The Divine Nature of Christ

The person of Jesus Christ is the Son of God, the Word, who, "before the world existed, had seen all things."[50] He is the "first principle of the universe," the creator of everything.[51] Thus the One who assumed humble flesh from the Virgin is also the One who is exalted in his divinity:

> He is, he is not, he is above being, he surpasses the being (*esse*) in all things,
> He reigns and possesses all, which he himself created;
> He is the whole through the whole (*totus per totum*),[52] who adheres to no parts;
> His highest nature is far apart from all things,
> since he is the simple, substantial essence of all things.
> He is the end and the beginning of all things that are beings.
> He is the Good (ἀγαθός) and the Beautiful (καλός), authentic Beauty (κάλλος), the figure of forms (μορφῶν χαρακτήρ);
> He is the one who calls wretched men back from eternal death,
> made man by assuming flesh from the Virgin,
> the Promised One, who came to fulfill the oracles of the prophets.[53]

When the Son assumed flesh from the Virgin, he did not abandon the characteristics of his divine nature. In this poem, Eriugena highlights the absolute transcendence and omnipotence of the divine Word, who is above all being. Yet he also stresses the immanence of the Word, "the whole through the whole," who sustains all being. In the Word, one finds the summation of all essential qualities—the Good, the Beautiful, etc.—, as well as the Truth of all forms, the primordial causes. This divine Son, who surpasses all things and is all things, is the same Son born of Mary, "the promised one."

In fact, the incarnate Word never abandons the fullness of his divinity, remaining always the Son in intimate union with the Father and the Spirit.

---

50. *Comm.* VI, i, 326, 2–7. This "seeing of all things" also includes all the Word's actions in the Incarnation: "For he himself knew, before the world came to be, all the miracles which he would do in the world." *Comm.* VI, i, 328, 30–31.

51. *Carm.* VIII, 86, 25–26.

52. The Word is in no way divided or diminished by his presence in all things.

53. *Carm.* VIII, 86, 31–40. God, the Creator of the universe, is "the highest honesty, the highest beauty (*pulchritudo*), the highest beatitude, the highest rest (*quies*), the highest happiness." *Peri.* V, 131, 4249–50. On the One as Beauty and Good see Rist, *Plotinus*, 53–65.

The *Alumnus* declares: "And though he has descended from the Father, he has not deserted the Father. He is always in the Father, since the Father is inseparably in him and he is inseparably in the Father."[54] Paradox does not deter Eriugena from proclaiming the truth: Jesus Christ is God in the flesh.

The continuity of the incarnate Word with his identity as the eternally begotten Son in the Trinity is therefore an essential truth for Eriugena. The reality of Christ's authentic humanity and the reality of his full divinity must be simultaneously maintained, as evinced by the two confessions of Peter and John: "Indeed Peter, recognizing Christ as God made man in time and saying: 'You are the Christ, the Son of the living God' (Matt 16:16), flew very high; but that other [John], who understood the same Christ to be God begotten of God before all the ages, said, 'In the beginning there was the Word' (John 1:1)."[55]

The One Christ: The Unity of the Two Natures

The unity of the two natures, divine and human, in the substance, or person, of Jesus realizes the union of grace and truth. The gift of human nature created in the image of God and elevated to glory, the grace, becomes one with the divinity of the only-begotten Son, the truth:

> "And we all received from his fullness" (John 1:16). Of which fullness is he speaking? None other than that of which he was speaking above: "And we saw his glory, the glory of the Only-Begotten of the Father, full of grace and truth" (John 1:14). Indeed, the fullness of *grace* dwells in Christ according his humanity and the fullness of *truth* according to his divinity. Thus the Apostle says: "In whom the fullness of divinity corporeally"—that is truly—"dwells" (Col 2:9). But how does the fullness of grace in Christ dwell according to his humanity? In no other way except that he himself is the first and greatest example of divine grace, because the man-Christ was assumed, by no previous merits, into the unity of substance (*substantia*) or, as it is more common to say, unity of person (*persona*). The fullness of truth, however, is in him naturally because he himself is truth, as when he himself testifies: "I am the way, the truth, and the life" (John 4:16).[56]

---

54. *Peri.* V, 73, 2327–30. Also see *Comm.* III, v, 222, 1–16.

55. *Hom.* III, 214–16, 15–19.

56. *Comm.* I, xxiv, 108–10, 1–16. Also see *Comm.* I, xxii, 102–4, 6–7; *Hom.* XXIII, 310–12, 1–15.

Eriugena affirms the hypostatic union, the union by "substance" or "person," and finds the roots of his affirmation in the Scriptures themselves. Yet he wants to highlight the effective nature of this miraculous union in the one person: in Jesus there is the grace of human nature restored and deified (he is the New Adam, "the first and greatest example of divine grace")[57] and, at the same time, there is the truth of the incomprehensible God.

The unity of the two natures in the single substance, or person, effects an exchange of characteristics without compromising either nature.[58] This "great exchange" results in a genuine descent of the Word with the simultaneous elevation of the flesh:

> What mind, what power, what created wisdom from above
> could speak of the descent of the Word into the flesh (*caro*),
> and know the sublime steps of the flesh into the Word?
> As the eternal God, made flesh, fell to the lower depths (*ima*),
> so the flesh, made truly God, lightly (*levis*) soars into the heights.[59]

So intimate is this exchange that, after the ascension, Jesus's human nature even shares in the divine characteristic of incomprehensibility:

> I, however, without hesitation follow in the footsteps of those who, without fear, preach that the humanity of our Lord Jesus Christ is united to his divinity, so that it is one—with the definitions (*ratio*) of the natures preserved—in itself and with itself, since the humanity and divinity of Christ are one substance, or, in common parlance, one person. And just as his divinity exceeds every intellect, so also his humanity is exalted and made superessential, above every visible and invisible creature, above all places and times, above every boundary and definition, above all the heavens, above all the virtues and powers, above everything which is said and understood, above everything which comes after God—it is incomprehensible and unknowable to every nature.[60]

Jesus unites the two natures and all the things contained in them. For this reason he is the angle that connects two creations: "Christ is the corner-stone, whom the perfidious Jews rejected, but was made the corner-stone

---

57. *Hom.* XXIII, 310, 9–12.

58. *Peri.* V, 221–22, 7190–96. The unity of two natures in Christ also distinguishes him from other men. John the Baptist, a *man* sent by God, is different from the One who is to come—Jesus, God and man. See *Hom.* XV, 274, 6–9; *Hom.* XV, 276, 17–18.

59. *Carm.* XXV, 118, 67–71.

60. *Peri.* V, 86, 2736–48.

for us. For in him the Church from Judea and the Church consisting of the Gentiles is joined. In him rational and intellectual, angelic nature and human, are made one. He is 'our peace who made two things one' (Eph 2:15). In him divinity and humanity, word and flesh, are made one substance in two natures."[61]

Eriugena holds that Jesus is "a man and more than a man."[62] By this expression he wishes to indicate the authenticity of Jesus's humanity, with all its strengths and weaknesses, and the fullness of Jesus's divinity, which surpasses all creatures. Jesus lives in solidarity with fallen humanity, but, at the same time, stands above all material and spiritual creation. He is, however, one subject, who, through a perfect union of natures and characteristics, lives in a divine-human manner. In reflecting on John 5:6—"Jesus, wearied as he was with his journey, sat down beside the well"—Eriugena beautifully highlights the paradoxical nature of the hypostatic union, in which the Word succumbs to exhaustion, while still reigning over all as "a man and more than a man."

> The fatigue of Jesus is his Incarnation. He assumed our nature, which, on account of Original Sin, was exhausted by the labors and toils of this world. His journey is the descent of his divinity in order to take up the likeness of our nature. He created us without labor through his divinity, and re-created us with labor through his humanity. Remaining eternally in himself and in his Father without change, he set out, so to speak, on a certain journey in the temporal dispensation through the flesh.[63]

The hypostatic union does not form a *tertium quid*: Jesus is not a hybrid, a mixture of divine and human. Yet though truly one with man, he is unique among creatures as the God-man. Jesus's divinity and humanity, exhaustion and glory, limitations and omnipotence, accessibility and incomprehensibility—all these paradoxes demonstrate the depths of God's love and desire to save man.

---

61. *Expo.* II, iv, 47, 1014–20.

62. John the Baptist compares himself to Jesus: "I, therefore, am a pure and simple man; he is more than a man, composed of humanity and divinity. He is Lord, I am a servant. He is king; I am the forerunner." *Comm.* I, xxiii, 106–8, 32–34.

63. *Comm.* IV, ii, 288, 21–41. Also see *Comm.* III, xi, 262, 4–10.

Conclusion

Eriugena's treatment of the *incarnatio,* the enfleshment of the divine Word, demonstrates a general knowledge of past controversies and councils. His conceptual vocabulary remains traditional, though it exhibits the desire to adapt Greek distinctions to Latin terminology (for example, *substantia* for *persona*). He clearly desires to demonstrate the truth of the *Logos's* descent through the authentic unification of the natures according to the Chalcedonian teachings: Jesus Christ is one substance [person] in two natures, true God and true man.

Eriugena restates and reformulates these positions not only to adhere to tradition, but also to establish the basis for creation's restoration and elevation to divine union. In the next chapter we shall examine more closely the underlying reasons for the coming of the God-made-man.

3

Cur Deus Homo?

ERIUGENA DOES NOT SETTLE UPON one reason alone for the Incarnation. Since the descent of the Word serves as a connecting thread throughout his works, one must pay close attention to discover its variety of implications. Soteriology, eschatology, sacramental theology, and ecclesiology—all of these themes find their principles in the mystery of Jesus Christ.

In this chapter, I would like to summarize and examine six reasons for the Word's descent. By taking into account a variety of sources—the *Periphyseon*, the Scripture commentaries, and the poetry—one can see both the traditional and the innovative in the Irishman's vision.

The Incarnation and Trinitarian Re-creation

The Incarnation affects a recreation of the cosmos: "He created us without labor through his divinity, he re-created us through labor in his humanity."[1] When man disobeyed God and chose to enjoy the fragmented vision of the effects in relation to himself, he shattered the unity of God's work and became ignorant of his own nature. Thus man's restoration to his pristine state—the potential paradise of his nature—requires a re-creation, a renewal of authentic man.

Just as the original creation of the eternal causes took place in the Word, so also must the re-creation of the fallen world come through the

1. *Comm.* IV, ii, 288, 26–27.

62

Word. The primordial voice of the Son echoes again in the Incarnation in order that he may proclaim the restorative truth within the fragmented effects:

> Thus the Word of God cries out in the remotest solitude of divine Goodness. His shout is the creation of all natures. For he himself calls those things which are as if they are not (Rom 4:17),[2] because God the Father cried out through him, that is, he created all things that he wanted to make. He cried out invisibly, before the world came to be, in order that the world might come to be. Coming into the world visibly, he cried out in order that the world might be saved. First he cried out eternally through his divinity alone, before the Incarnation; he cried out afterwards through his flesh.[3]

One should not, however, understand the re-creation in the incarnate Word apart from the Trinity. In fact, the re-creation that comes from the descent of the Word into the effects recapitulates that which took place in the hidden recesses of the Godhead. Eriugena makes a parallel between the Trinitarian action in the "first creation" and the Trinitarian action of restoration through the Incarnation. In formulating the parallel, he draws from the Scriptures and Christian tradition. Eriugena understands creation and restoration to take place through the unified immanent and economic Trinity.

Creation in the Immanent Trinity

In the Trinity, the Father forms all natures in their causes: "Thus I believe that theology attributes the property of the creation of the natures causally to God the Father. For 'In the beginning, God made heaven and earth' (Gen 1:1)."[4] The primordial causes have their origin in the Father, the *source* of all things. This eternal establishment of all things in their unity takes place invisibly, since the causes still lack being, that is, they cannot yet be perceived or known by any intellect.

The causes move from the inscrutable darkness of the Father to the light of God the Son, the Word. The Son is the field of the first creation, the

---

2. Eriugena changes the verse to fit his distinctions of being and non-being. See *Comm.*, 142, n. 20.

3. *Comm.* I, xxviii, 142, 92–101.

4. *Peri.* II, 50, 1157–59.

receiver of the hidden causes of the Father. He gives them substance and truth in himself:

> The Scriptures assert, however, that the substantive reasons of all things are created in the Word, as previously mentioned examples attest: "In the beginning God made heaven and earth" (Gen 1:1), and "You made all things in Wisdom" (Ps 104:24). For "the beginning" is not one thing, "Wisdom" another, and "the Word" another, but all these names signify the only-begotten Son of God, in whom and through whom the Father made all things. Again, the Apostle says: "In whom we live and move and have our being" (Acts 17:28).[5]

The eternal Son of God is Creative Wisdom through his *receptivity*. He receives the gift of the Father—the eternal reasons or causes—and gives this gift substance in himself. This movement from Father to Son should not be understood in terms of temporal succession, but rather as a logical perception of the priority in the unified substance of the Trinity: the Father is *source*, the Son is the *receiver*.[6] One cannot yet perceive this movement of creation, however, since it remains hidden within the intimate relationship between Father and Son.[7]

The substantive causes in the Word move from their hidden unity into their various species through the *distribution* of the Holy Spirit:

> We find that the same *theologia* applies the distribution of all the causes, which the Father created universally and essentially in His Word, truly to the Holy Spirit. For if the Apostle says that

5. *Peri.* II, 50, 1163–68. On the primordial causes in the Trinity see Beirwaltes, "Unity and Trinity," 219–20.

6. In a certain sense the primordial causes are coeternal with the maker—they cannot be "accidental" to God, since this would complicate divine simplicity. Yet the priority of the Maker means that causes can never be coeternal with God in the truest sense. The *Alumnus* says: "For we certainly believe that the Son is coeternal with the Father and those things which the Father made in the Son are coeternal with the Son, but not, however, entirely coeternal. For they are coeternal because the Son was never without the primordial causes of natures made in him. But these causes are not entirely coeternal with him in whom they are made. For it is not possible for made things to be coeternal with the Maker. For the Maker precedes that which he makes." *Peri.* II, 48, 1116–22.

7. Nature includes things "that are" (perceptible by the mind) and things "that are not" (transcendent and ineffable). This means that the term signifies not only the theophany of creation, but also God and the primordial causes in the Word. The term nature therefore expresses the intimate union of Creator, causes, and effects, while allowing for the essential distinctions. On Eriugena's use of the term see O'Meara, "Concept of *Natura*," 139.

the partition and distribution of divine gifts are given to the Holy Spirit (Isa 11:1–3), why wouldn't the division of the primordial causes created substantially in the Word of God also be attributed to the Holy Spirit? . . . We are able to demonstrate this also from the *Book of Genesis*: "The Spirit of God brooded upon the waters" (Gen 1:2). For what else are we to understand regarding the Spirit of God brooding over, fecundating, and nourishing the waters of the primordial causes, than that the Spirit distributes and orders those things which were made uniformly, unified, and simply in the Word, into the differences in genus, form, wholes and parts, and all the numbers?[8]

The Holy Spirit, therefore, is the *distributor* of the fruitfulness of the causes in the Word.[9] Through the Spirit, the potential being of every essence finds its own voice.

Re-creation in the Economic Trinity

Humanity's fall into sin, however, called for the radical descent of the Word in the Incarnation. Man's broken nature shattered the unity of creation itself, dragging all things into corruption and fragmentation. The enfleshment of the Word, as God's response to the fall, led to the restoration of human nature and the elevation of creation to divine unity through grace.

The enfleshment of the Word reshapes the Trinitarian relations in the economy. In the original creation, the Father is the *source* or cause; the Son is the *receiver* of the causes and gives them substance; and the Holy Spirit is the *distributor* of these causes into their variety in unity. When the Word becomes flesh, however, a new order is established. The Word continues his mission as the receiver, but, instead of accepting the primordial causes from the Father, he now receives the sevenfold restorative gifts—Wisdom, Understanding, Counsel, Knowledge, Fortitude, Piety, Fear of the Lord—from the Holy Spirit in order to distribute them to the church for the healing of the faithful. "For the Spirit," writes Eriugena, "itself is coessential with the Son according to divinity, over whom the Spirit causes the divine gifts, which it distributes, to rest according to [the Son's] humanity. . . . The head of the Church, that is, Christ, receives all these spirits, that is, all the gifts

8. *Peri.* II, 50–51, 1170–75; 1182–88.

9. The relations of the Trinitarian persons in creation reflect the Neoplatonic triad of being (Father), Wisdom (Son), and Life (the Spirit). See *Peri.* I, 23, 575–78.

of the Spirit, first according to his humanity, and then he distributes them through his spirit to his Church."[10] The Son humbles himself in becoming man, enters the created order, and becomes the recipient of transformative virtues on behalf of the church.

The Father, however, remains the source of these seven-fold restorative gifts and gives them to the Holy Spirit for distribution to the Son in order that they might have being in the life of the church. None of the faithful, writes Eriugena, "doubts that these [gifts] come from any other place than from the cause of all goods, I mean from the Father."[11] Therefore, through the Incarnation a new order is established: the Father remains the *source*, but the Holy Spirit *distributes* the seven gifts in the church through the *receiver*, the enfleshed Word.[12]

The historical Incarnation of the Word forms these relations of the Trinity within the economy, since Christ is the builder (*fabricator*) and head of the church.[13] The Word truly becomes man and acquires a divine-human relationship with the Spirit and the Father, allowing him to effect the recreation of the fallen cosmos. Jesus now receives the healing gifts to distribute in his body, the church, which finds life, restoration, and elevation through these seven-fold virtues.[14]

The Restoration of the Pre-lapsarian Nature

The recreation of the cosmos begins, therefore, with man. The incarnate Word, however, is not simply the locus for the distribution of the Spirit's restorative gifts. He also refashions man according to his pristine, pre-lapsarian nature. God became enfleshed "in order to save [human nature] and call it back to its original state."[15] Jesus is the "Second Man" through whom the "First Man"—fallen humanity—receives new life.[16] Without the return of man through Christ, creation itself would remain in its devastation.

10. *Peri.* II, 52, 1206–9; 1213–16. Also see *Comm.* III, xii, 272, 30–34.

11. *Peri.* II, 53, 1229–36.

12. On this point also see Mooney, "Leuchter," 574–75.

13. See *Comm.* III, xii, 272, 30–34; IV, i, 282, 59–68.

14. Christ, the Bridegroom, came for the sake of the church (*propter ecclesiam venit*). See *Comm.* III, x, 258, 7–21.

15. *Peri.* IV, 116, 3489–92. Also see *Peri.* V, 165, 5393–95; *Expo.* IV, iv, 81–82, 674–78.

16. One of the punishments of the devil is seeing the First Man, Adam, receive rewards through the death of the Second Man, Christ. See *Peri.* V, 207, 6699–6702.

The resurrection and the ascension of Christ, as we shall see, are essential for the return of man. In the raising and elevation of Jesus, all of human nature receives its liberation from the weight of the material body and enters into the intended state of the spiritual body. Taking his cue from Maximus the Confessor, Eriugena teaches that the return to paradise in Christ means a simplification of human nature and an elimination of deleterious distinctions, as symbolized by the resolution of the divisions of male and female. Through Christ, earth and paradise are joined in order that "there be no diversity of parts in them and all will be Paradise."[17]

The Incarnation, through the resurrection, liberates the body from the weight of matter and returns it to the authentic state of spirit. Eriugena takes literally Jesus's promise that man shall be "like the angels," since through Christ man will become one with the angels in nature. "For it is not inappropriate to believe that the first condition of man before sin in paradise, that is, in the heavenly beatitude, was equal to the angels and connatural with them."[18]

Saving the Effects through Man

Just as man brought about the deleterious dispersion of the effects into a conflicting variety, so he becomes the mediator of their return to harmonious unity. The Word, by restoring human nature, allows man, the "workshop of the world," to fulfill the mission for which he was created:

> Since the whole world in its species (*specialiter*) is even now restored in the only-begotten and incarnate, Word of God made man (*inhumanato*), truly it will be restored in Him universally and generally at the end of the world. For that which he perfects as a species (*specialiter*) in himself, he will perfect generally in all—and I mean not only in all men, but also in every sensible creature. Indeed, the Word of God himself, when he assumed human nature, did not pass over any created substance, which he did not assume in his human nature. Therefore, in assuming human nature, he assumed every creature. For this reason, if he saved and restored

17. *Peri.* II, 14, 250–52. Also see Maximus, *Ambigua* XLI, 1305D.

18. *Peri.* II, 67, 1536–39. On being equal to the angels (*isangelos*) see Clemens, *Stromateis* VII, x, 186–88, 16–26; Origenes, *Contra Celsum* IV, xxix, 252, 16–26; Gregorius Nyssenus, *De virginitate* IV, iv, 442, 15–20; Maximus, *Ambigua* XLI, 1308A–B.

human nature, which he received, he has restored perfectly every visible and invisible creature.[19]

In this passage, Eriugena highlights two important aspects of the salvation of the effects in man. First, man and the effects in him already enjoy the benefits of the Word's condescension. Though the general return has not yet taken place, nonetheless it already has its assurance in Christ, who sustains all things in himself. The Incarnation has implications for the present and not just for the future.

Second, all things will return universally and generally to unity through the Word's re-creation of human nature in the Incarnation. In effect, the Incarnation allows human nature to fulfill its created role: to be the unifier of creation. "Indeed human nature is whole in the whole of all created nature, since in it every creature was established and in it every creature was joined, and into it every creature will return, and through it every creature must be saved. . . . Everything that was naturally created in man remains, by necessity, eternally whole and uncorrupted. For by divine justice it is not right that anything should perish from that which [God] has made, especially since nature itself did not sin, but [man's] perverse will [sinned], which moves irrationally against rational nature."[20] In fact, even the angels will be part of this general return in man, since man also includes spirit in himself.[21] The Incarnation saves *all* creatures, on earth and in heaven, by letting man perform his divinely intended role.

The Redemption of Man and the Destruction of Sin

Eriugena often writes of the Incarnation as both the liberation of man from sin and the expression of divine justice. God permits creation's fall as a just punishment for sin, since it is a period in which man must do penance for his transgression.[22] The suffering that man experiences in his broken

19. *Peri.* V, 74, 2361–72.

20. *Peri.* IV, 27–28, 723–26; 742–47.

21. See *Peri.* V, 75, 2373–91.

22. While John the Baptist represents this time of penance for man, Jesus is the enfleshment of the divine justice that will bring an end to sin's reign. "John is the figure of penance, since he preached penance; Christ, however, is the figure of justice, not only because he judges the world, but also because he is eternal justice. Penance does not generally come about except after the transgression of justice. Thus human nature, which transgressed the divine laws in paradise, preaches and does penance in the person of

nature inspires conversion and a return to truth. Yet it also leads him to the grace offered in the person of Jesus Christ, who has come "to dissolve the servitude of the visible creature."[23]

In treating these themes, Eriugena draws upon traditional categories, but develops them within his understanding of man's fall and return. Man's freedom from sin and death depends upon Jesus's passion and cross, Jesus's defeat of the devil, and Jesus's continuous, liberating action upon the believer.

The Reign of Evil

Man now finds himself mired in sin. For Eriugena, sin and its companion, death, are "non-being"[24] that mar the unity of nature. Evil itself is not a thing, but a perversion of the Good. It "is surrounded by the form of the Good, but in itself it is without form and incomprehensible; it is neither from God nor from any other certain and defined cause. Indeed, evil is variable and uncaused, since it is not found in the nature of things in any substantial way."[25] While sin and evil emerge from man's misuse of his

John. It [human nature] declares clearly that the substantial justice of the Word of God precedes it according to divinity, and that [the substantial justice of the Word of God] will come after it according to the dispensation of the flesh. This takes place in order that the Word might recall it—I'm speaking of human nature—to the pristine state of eternal justice through living according to the divine laws, which it had spurned out of pride." *Comm.* I, xxix, 150, 9–20.

23. *Peri.* V, 109, 3469–70. Eriugena presents the "certitude of God's redemptive intention in His creation, and of man's capability of embracing this intention." Wohlman, *Philosopher,* 648.

24. One should not confuse this sense of non-being with the non-being of divine transcendence. This point is important to Eriugena's argument against double predestination: God is the cause of things that are, not of things that "are not," that is, sin. "God, however, is the cause of those things which are. Therefore, he is not the cause of things that are not. Sin and its effect, death accompanied by misery, 'are not.' Therefore neither God nor predestination, which he is, can be the cause of these things." *Prae.* III, iii, 21, 89–93. Also see *Prae.* II, iii, 20, 66.

25. *Peri.* IV, 123, 3705–9. That evil has "no cause," that it is unintelligible, is a theme of late Neoplatonism, which Eriugena acquired from pseudo-Dionysius. See Dionysius, *De divinis nominibus* IV, xxii, 177, 7–15. Eric Perl rightly notes the implications of this idea: "To explain evil, to attribute a cause to it, would necessarily be to explain it away, to deny that evil is genuinely evil at all. For to explain something is to show how it is in some way good. 'Tout comprendre, c'est tout pardonner'. Only by *not* explaining evil, by insisting rather on its radical causelessness, its unintelligibility, can we take evil seriously as evil. This is why most 'theodicies' fail precisely insofar as they succeed." Perl, *Theophany,*

nature, they remain unintelligible because they are without substance and "known" only as a perversion of the Good.

As we have already seen, Eriugena does not believe that matter is evil; yet matter and sensory experience are the hosts of evil. Sin and evil certainly emerge from man's irrational will, but they feed upon the weighted qualities that surround man's material body after the fall. The authentic nature of man—the soul-spiritual body composite—remains intact, preserved by Christ; but the fallen, "exterior" nature of man—the carnal body—experiences uncertainty and ruin:

> For truth and every good lives in the interior man, which is the Word of God, the only-begotten Son, our Lord Jesus Christ, outside of whom there is no good, since He himself is every truth and substantial good and goodness. And evil and malice are opposed to him from the other side. And because every evil is not found substantially in the nature of things, nor does it come from any certain or natural cause—for in itself it is considered entirely nothing, except as an irrational, perverse, and imperfect motion of rational nature—it finds no other basis in the universal creature, except where falsity possesses it. The proper possession of falsity, however, is corporeal sense. For no other part of human nature receives the error of falsity, except the exterior sense; indeed through it [exterior sense], the interior sense, reason, and even intellect itself very often fall into error.[26]

Eriugena's understanding of sin and evil, therefore, exonerates nature and places the blame upon the misuse of man's will: "For this reason the cause of evil is not established in nature itself, but in the intemperance of those who abuse nature."[27] Nature deserves to be saved, while the parasitical perversion of sin and evil, which feed upon the weight of carnal experience, must be canceled for the return to occur. "For it is not appropriate for divine justice that anything that [God] made should perish, especially since nature itself did not sin, but the perverse will sinned, which is moved irrationally against rational nature."[28]

---

63. Furthermore, if one gives a cause to evil, one establishes a connection between cause and effect, thereby making evil "necessary" in creation.

26. *Peri.* IV, 120, 3610–23.

27. *Peri.* IV, 144, 4409–10.

28. *Peri.* IV, 28, 744–47.

The Salvific Passion and Death of Jesus

The Word became incarnate in order to suffer and die for the liberation of man and all creation from sin and death. On the one hand, the cross represents a genuine sacrifice that takes place to eradicate sin: "For who would doubt that sacrifice (*hostia*) and sin are opposed to one another, for a sacrifice occurs for no other reason than the destruction of sin. Christ is the general sacrifice for the sin of the whole world."[29] The Word is "redemption, salvation, purgation, illumination, and the perfection of the whole of humanity in all things and in particulars."[30]

On the other hand, Eriugena expands the sacrificial dimension of Christ's death to include the themes of re-creation and recapitulation: Jesus, on the cross, liberates creation from sin through a reformation of the fallen cosmos.

The Transitus of the Cross: Re-creation

Transitus—"passage" or "transition"—stands out as a key theological and philosophical concept in Eriugena's works. It is a term of biblical provenance, established by the Lord himself: "Heaven and earth will pass away (*transibunt*), but my words will not pass away" (Mark 13:31).[31] This passage of the world, however, embraces a number of transitions that shape the re-creation of the cosmos.

In a physical sense, matter makes a *transitus,* or change, from one species to another.[32] More importantly, however, the future return of all things to divine unity marks a series of passages (*transitus*) from a lower state of being to a higher: from bodies to souls; from souls to primordial causes; from the primordial causes to divine unity.[33] In this succession of passages, nothing is annihilated, but rather a substance remains constant in its ascent to a higher and more authentic state: a *transitus* is a movement

---

29. *Prae.* IX, iv, 59, 95–97. Here Eriugena is commenting on 2 Cor 5:21: "He who did not know sin was made sin for our sake."

30. *Peri.* V, 170, 5532–36.

31. On the Lord's use of *transitus* see *Peri.* V, 44–45, 1391–1408.

32. *Peri.* V, 104, 3297–3302.

33. *Peri.* V, 25, 718–21.

from brokenness to restoration.[34] All things will pass (*transiturum*) "from earthly qualities to heavenly qualities, like smoke that turns into a flame."[35]

One may also make passages to higher levels of transformative knowledge and experience. Man, in cooperation with divine grace, rises to ever deeper forms of divine union: "The first *transitus* is of the mind (*animus*) into the knowledge of all things that come after God; the second is of knowledge into wisdom, that is, the intimate contemplation of the truth, in so far as it is permitted to a creature; and the third, and highest, is the movement of the purest souls supernaturally into God and into the darkness of the incomprehensible and inaccessible light, in which the causes of all things are hidden."[36] The contemplation of the Scriptures, in particular, facilitates this ascent as the believer passes from the carnal to the spiritual.[37]

In *Carmina* Three, an Easter poem,[38] Eriugena portrays the passion, death, resurrection, and ascension of Christ as a *transitus* that recreates the fallen cosmos. The celebration of Easter, in fact, recapitulates the divine passages that occur in the creative act and in the economy. He begins by depicting the passage from nothing to the visible cosmos, that is, from the hidden causes in God to the comprehensible theophany of creation:

> It is said that the *passage (transitus)* of the framework of the world
> moved fully from nothing into the particular species.
> The Creator, who held the causes always in himself,
> brought them forth into the forms that were visible in the light.[39]

34. "For this same reason I think that corporeal substance will pass into soul, not that what it is may perish, but that it may be preserved in a better essence." *Peri.* V, 28, 838–41. Also see *Peri.* V, 167–68, 5458–68. Werner Beierwaltes discusses the significance of the term in dialectic and in the expression of God's *exitus* and *reditus* in the making of creation. See Beierwaltes, *Grundzüge*, 71–72.

35. *Peri.* V, 177, 5773–83.

36. *Peri.* V, 225, 7312–18.

37. "What is this passage (*transitus*), O Lord, if not the ascent through the infinite steps of contemplation [of the Scriptures]? For you make a passage (*transitus*) in the intellects of those seeking and finding you." *Peri.* V, 210–11, 6828–31. Also see *Comm.* VI, vi, 360, 36–40. On the exegetical significance of *transitus* in Tyconius see Jeauneau, "Pseudo-Dionysius," 149.

38. The dating of this poem is uncertain. Charles was present at the liturgy that the poem commemorates. See *Carm.*, 138, n. Poem 3.

39. *Carm.* III, 68, 5–8.

This first *tranistus* is God's *exitus*. The creation from nothing—God's incomprehensible self—takes place in the movement from the eternal causes to the unified diversity of the world.

Next, he describes the *transitus* that occurs within the fallen state of creation. God acts in history in order to bring the corrupted cosmos back to its blessed origins. This is the Pasch—the flight of the Israelites from slavery and God's punishment of the Egyptians—that impresses the economy with the pattern of divine liberation from oppression:

> Moses, the leader of the people, celebrated the second Pasch,
> cutting down Isis with a twice-five blow.
> The Lord *passed over (transivit)* the posts marked with blood,
> while Egypt herself mourned her first born.[40]

Christ, however, recapitulates and fulfills these passages through his own victory upon the cross and his ascent to the Father. In this third *transitus*, he bears all things in himself as both God and man:

> These things were once signs of the Christ to come,
> in whom the things long hidden shine forth together.
> He alone was victor, when the Prince of the World was laid low;
> he leapt forth from Erebus when the third day had passed.
> And first trampling death he *passed through (transivit)* into the heavens,
> for he alone was free from Tartarus's power.
> Pouring forth libations of his own blood
> he dedicates the new Pasch to the world that has been saved.[41]

This poem, therefore, follows the transitions that establish the creation and re-creation of all things. These passages, however, depend upon the fulfillment that takes place in the incarnate Word and his sacrificial death: the Word's body dies and is raised, thereby opening the *transitus* of creation from the carnal to the authentic spiritual state. The on-going relevance of Christ's passion and death becomes evident when Eriugena describes an implicit fourth *transitus* in the celebration of the Easter liturgy:

> Now the sacred symbols of these realities are celebrated,
> when things known previously by the mind appear before our eyes;
> when the pious mind through the heart knows the body of Christ
> and the wave of his sacred blood as the price for the world;

40. *Carm.* III, 68, 25–28.
41. *Carm.* III, 69, 45–52.

when remembering we recall the Supper of the Lord for years;
when the choir itself sings with many hymns.[42]

When the believer participates in the liturgy, he or she experiences a passage from symbol to reality: one moves from the mind—knowledge of God's creation and salvation history—to the heart, the transforming experience of re-creation and ascent.[43] The Christian becomes part of the mystery of the Word's *exitus* and *reditus* in the cross, resurrection, and ascension.

The "Six Ages" and the Cross: Recapitulation

In his commentary on John 4:5–6,[44] Eriugena adapts Augustine's interpretation of Jesus's stop for rest near the well of Jacob at the "sixth hour." Augustine interprets the six hours as an allegory for the six ages of the world:

> So why the sixth hour then? Because it is the sixth age of the world. In the Gospel, count from Adam up to Noah as one hour, one age; a second from Noah up to Abraham; a third from Abraham up to David; a fourth from David to the exile in Babylon; a fifth from the exile in Babylon up to the baptism of John; from then on the sixth is running its course.
>
> Why be surprised? Jesus came and, humbling himself, he came to the well. He came weary, because he carried the weakness of the flesh. He came at the sixth hour, because it was the sixth age of the world. He came to a well, because he came into the very depths of this dwelling place of ours—which is why it says in the psalms, "Out of the depths have I cried to you, Lord" (Ps 129:1). He sat down, as I said, because he humbled himself.[45]

---

42. *Carm.* III, 69, 61–66.

43. On the Eucharistic celebration and spiritual participation see *Comm.* VI, vi, 364–66, 82–96. On Eriugena's treatment of the sacraments see Walker, "Sacraments," 156–58.

44. "So he came to a city of Samaria, called Sychar, near the field that Jacob gave to his son Joseph. Jacob's well was there, and so Jesus, wearied as he was with his journey, sat down beside the well. It was about the sixth hour."

45. Augustinus, *In Ihoannis Evangelium*, XV, ix, 153–54, 1–11 (Hill translation, 280). Augustine offers other historical schemas that include a seventh—the eternal rest—or even the eighth—the fulfillment of all things in Christ—day or age. See Augustinus, *De Genesi contra Manicheos*, I, xxiii, *xxxv–xl*, 104–11; *De diversis questionibus* LVIII, ii, 105–7, 26–82; *De Catichizandis* XVII, xxviii–xxxii, *xxxix*, 152–164; *De Trinitate* IV, ii, iv, 169–71. Also see Daley, *Hope*, 133–35; de Lubac, *Catholicism*, 152; Luneau, *L'histoire*, 379–83; van Oort, "The End," 3.

For Augustine, the six hours represent the six ages, beginning with the creation of man. This passage of time is the debilitating, wearying ages of the flesh. Jesus inaugurates the sixth age with the start of his public mission, that is, his baptism in the Jordan by John. This sixth age has not yet ended— it is still "running its course"—and is, therefore, a time of anticipation: Jesus began this final age and will conclude it when he comes again.

Eriugena assumes Augustine's basic interpretation of the six hours as six ages, but makes significant changes:

> "It was around the sixth hour." The sixth hour prefigures the sixth age of the world. The first age is calculated from the expulsion of the first man from paradise up to the altar, which Noah, exiting from the ark, constructed after the flood (Gen 8:20); the second, from then up to the altar, upon which Abraham was ordered by God to sacrifice Isaac (Gen 22:1–14); the third, from then up to the altar of king David on the threshing floor of Ornan the Jebusite (1 Chr 21:18); then the fourth, up to the altar of Zorobabel in the reconstructed temple (Esd 3:2–3); then the fifth, up to the baptism of John, or, as it does not seem unreasonable to many, up to the true altar, that is, up to the cross of Christ, of which all the previous altars were types. Thus the sixth age is extended to the end of the world; it is taking place now. For the seventh age is perfected in another life in the souls liberated from their bodies, which begins from the martyrdom of Abel and will terminate at the end of the world with the resurrection of all. After this, the eighth age begins to appear, which no termination can enclose. The perfected light of grace is also symbolized typically in the sixth hour, which, when Christ became man, fully shone in the world. Six, therefore, is a perfect number.[46]

A comparison between Eriugena's eight ages and Augustine's six reveals some significant points. First, for Eriugena, history begins not from the creation of Adam, but from the moment of Adam's expulsion. This is consistent with Eriugena's understanding of the fall and the nature of the fragmented existence of creation: the calculation of history—the movement of man in time—begins only with man's separation from God and pristine human nature's expulsion from paradise.[47] History is, above all, the story of man's fall and return.

46. *Comm.* IV, ii, 288–90, 42–61.

47. "That particular Adam would not have been born into this corruptible world through generation, if the fault of human nature had not preceded." *Comm.* I, xxxi, 174, 49–51. Also see Jeauneau, *Comm.*, 290, n. 7.

More importantly, Eriugena marks the ages not only by particular biblical figures, but also by the construction of altars. Each age finds its closure and beginning in the performance of sacrifice: Noah's altar, Abraham's altar, David's altar, and Zorobabel's altar. This allows him to adopt a typological structure that finds its fulfillment in the true altar: the cross of Jesus Christ. In fact, Jesus's passion and death recapitulate salvation history and inaugurate the sixth age—a break from Augustine, who sees the sixth age beginning with the public ministry of Jesus (the baptism of John). The cross, therefore, establishes the stage of historical waiting, since the victory of Jesus's passion and resurrection ensures the inauguration of the eighth day of the general resurrection and divine union.

Finally, Eriugena's conception of history includes a waiting period, the seventh age, that exists outside of historical time, but paradoxically remains connected to the other six ages. The seventh age is, in effect, the "intermediate state" of souls between individual death and the general resurrection. It begins with a historical event, the death of Abel, the just martyr, and will end simultaneously with the sixth age.[48] Therefore, even the intermediate state depends upon the cross for its fulfillment, since the cross's effects transcend the limitations of temporal progression: without the sacrifice of Christ and the resurrection from the dead, even the just dead of the past cannot find rest. All the ages find their fulfillment in Jesus's salvific death.

The cross, for Eriugena, marks a decisive point in history and extends its embrace even to the transtemporal. It recapitulates the frustrated sacrifices of salvation history and fulfills them in the definitive end of the ages: the eighth day, the day without end.

Christ's Exchange for the Life of the World

In his poetry, Eriugena portrays the death of Jesus as an "exchange": the death of Jesus for the life of the world. The wonder of this exchange, however, lies in the fact that, after the resurrection, Jesus holds the purchase (the life of the world) and the price (his own life) at the same time. It is an exchange without loss to the purchaser:

> He freely laid down his soul and took it up again.
> That which he was able to put down, he did not allow to remain.
> That which he gave for the life of the world, he called back.

---

48. On the intermediate state see *Peri.* V, 194–95, 6315–18.

That which is given is received; that which was handed over
remains safe.
Oh wonderful to tell! Such a price is given for the world:
All is saved, all is restored and given back.
Who can say what the Redeemer himself has done?
He holds the purchase, he possesses the price.[49]

Jesus freely makes this great exchange. He is the willing priest and victim; he lays down his soul and recalls it; he is the victor who loses nothing of himself and restores the world. The host that is "pleasing to the Father" affects the resurrection and the defeat of death.

The sign of the cross conveys the full sweep of the incarnate Word's salvific purchase. The cross liberates humanity and leaves the faithful free from the harm of the world.[50] It redeems and restores all of creation, from the humblest of creatures to the angelic hosts:

Look upon the orb bright with the sun's rays,
which the salvific cross spreads from its height.
It holds the earth and sea, the winds and the heavens,
and anything else above that is believed to be far away.

The angels, archangels, princes and all beings above,
the celestial host, seeking the heights, worships you [the cross].
Our Church praises you [the cross] from here with appropriate song
for through you, O Christ-Bearer, it was redeemed.[51]

The cross, the Christ-Bearer (*christifera*), receives its power and glory through the gift of the incarnate Word. It is the locus of the Lord's victory over sin and death and, therefore, the salvation of man and the restorer of the world.

Defeating the Devil

Jesus defeats the devil through the exchange of his sacrifice: "For just as the blood of Christ aided men in their redemption and will accomplish the restoration of man's original nature, so also it harms the devil and his

---

49. *Carm.* VI, 80, 25–32.

50. *Expo.* VIII, ii, 128, 376–77.

51. *Carm.* II, 64, 1–4; 11–14. Hilary Richardson notes the possible influence of the Celtic cross, with its surrounding orb, upon this poem. Richardson, "Themes," 265.

angels, bringing about the destruction of their empire, and it will harm them through the increase of their punishment."[52]

Clearly Eriugena's adherence to the Neoplatonic schema of descent and return does not lead him to reject the notion of man's captivity by the devil. The descent of the incarnate word into the effects initiates the return to unity, but through the defeat of the Prince of the World. Humanity needs Jesus for its liberation from the dominion of Satan, the serpent, who rules through the characteristics of man's fallen state: man's false "prudence of the flesh" and man's "empty and false wisdom."[53]

God, according to Eriugena, did not create the devil and his mignons in their evil state, for in the beginning they were good angels. Their wickedness comes from the perversion of their wills and their assumption of base characteristics through the fall. The devil remains a "divine creation," despite the destruction wrought by his hand.[54] His original goodness and the dignity "of his primal condition, before he became proud and seduced man, remains, and will remain, forever and unchanged, apart from any diminution in it."[55]

Yet the devil is a formidable enemy who must be overthrown. Eriugena's most important reflections upon the defeat of Satan appear in three poems on the "Harrowing of Hell" (*Carmina* 6, 7, 9). In these hymns, Jesus descends into Satan's realm and defeats the tyrant and seducer of man. In *Carmina* Six, he describes this victory in graphic images:

> But the tyrant did not escape through the dark caves:
> a stronger one than he had entered, who took away his vessels.

52. *Peri.* V, 199, 6442–46.

53. *Peri.* IV, 153, 4709–13.

54. "Why, however, is this dragon [the devil], with all the evil members who follow his evil, called a spiritual formation (*formatio*) or image (*figmentum*) of God? It may be understood in two ways. First, it is because all the apostate angels and all their human followers, in so far as they naturally exist, were created by God, and therefore it is not inappropriate to believe that they are a formation or image of God. Second, that such symbolic words in such sentences of the divine scripture did not always signify the nature of demons and evil men, in which the creator of all good things established them. Instead, they signify those things which were superadded to the essence established in them on account of the disobedience of each one—characteristics such as the aerial bodies of demons and the terrestrial and mortal members of men, which must be believed and understood to have been superadded without delay as a punishment for sin to the simple nature created by God." *Peri.* IV, 157, 4820–34.

55. *Peri.* V, 113, 3625–30. Eriugena refuses to speculate on the possible return of the devil. See *Peri.* V, 113, 3632–35.

He was dragged away, captured, conquered, and bound in chains,
restrained, overcome, struck down from his thrown,
on which previously he, the Prince of the World, had once sat
from on high
—the savage and voracious beast, who had been for so long
unconquered.
But the conqueror of the world, alone and more powerful than all,
struck the beast down and beat in his head.[56]

Christ overthrows Satan and his kingdom in a genuine battle that frees the captive souls from hell. This triumph establishes a new order in which sin and death no longer hold sway.

The devil effectively destroys himself by falling for the deception of the incarnate Word. In attempting to devour the source of life, the Prince of the World allowed Christ to enter his kingdom and destroy it from within. Satan himself proclaims his woes in *Carmina* Nine:

I see myself conquered, a fugitive from the dark abodes.
What is the new light arising that I shall never be able to bear?

I confess that I did this! I caused it all!
His virtue and humble power lay hidden from me, a fool!
If I had known this, he would never have hung upon the cross;
The servile form of the human body deceived me![57]

The Son defeats Satan through the material, mortal body that he had assumed in the Incarnation. His divinity, veiled by his humble appearance, dupes the torturer of man and reclaims the world for the divine gift of life. Eriugena adopts these traditional themes, demonstrating that the incarnate Word freely gave himself in order that the devil's reign of sin and death might end.

The Incarnation as Effective Theophany

Man's dilemma after the fall lies in the fact that his ignorance of self and his fragmented perception of creation impede his role as the unifier of all things. He cannot see creation *in God*, he can only see creation in reference *to himself*. Mired in the swamp of unstable temporal and sensory deceptions, he has become the obstacle to the return. Man, therefore, must

---

56. *Carm.* VI, 80, 9–16.
57. *Carm.* IX, 92, 37–38; 47–50.

see God the Trinity in order to perceive creation as it truly is: God's self-creation from nothing and the simple Truth of all that exists.

The Incomprehensible God and Theophanies

The problem of "seeing God" has a long history in Christian thought: how can one see or define the One who is above all descriptions or limitations?[58] As we have noted, Eriugena emphasizes the invisibility and ineffability of God to the point of calling God "non-being," that is, God "is not" because he cannot be perceived by any created intellect.[59] No creature may grasp the mystery of the Triune God: "Yet by no means is [knowledge of the generation of the Son from the Father] in me or in the angel as vision. For, 'Who will tell of his generation' (Isa 53:8)? For no man, no celestial power, is able to know the generation of the Word from the Father—how it takes place or what it is."[60] God is without definition, outside of any borders that would render him comprehensible.[61]

For this reason, intellectual creatures require theophanies in order to know *that* God exists and *that* God is Trinity. A theophany, according to Eriugena, is the "appearance of that which does not appear, the manifestation of the hidden, the affirmation of the negation, the comprehension of the incomprehensible, the enunciation of the ineffable."[62] These paradoxes indicate that a theophany both illuminates and, at the same time, veils the divine. A theophany genuinely manifests God, but it should never be equated with God.[63]

The first theophany of God is creation itself. In choosing to create, God comes out of the darkness and makes himself known. According to Eriugena "theophanies are the species of visible and invisible things. Through their order and beauty God is known to be: one does not discover

58. For example see Origenes, *De principiis,* I, i, *vi,* 100; Gregorius Nyssenus, *De beatitudinibus* VI, 139, 14–21; 140, 5–8.

59. *Peri.* III, 24, 638–41.

60. *Peri.* II, 43, 1007–11.

61. See *Peri.* II, 84, 1983–92.

62. *Peri.* III, 22, 589–92.

63. Eriugena likens a theophany to the movement of the human intellect from its hiddenness into discernible acts. "And when our intellect appears extrinsically, it always remains intrinsically invisible; and when it leaps forth into various forms comprehensible to the senses, it never abandons the incomprehensible state of its nature; and before it is made evident exteriorly, it moves itself within itself." *Peri.* III, 22–23, 603–7.

what he is, but only *that* he is, since the nature itself of God is neither expressed nor understood. The inaccessible light surpasses every intellect."[64] In all created things "that which is invisible in itself appears."[65] One may contemplate God through what God has made, keeping in mind that what God has made can neither truly reveal God nor "be" God.

Creation, however, manifests God to different degrees. The higher one goes through the hierarchy of beings, the greater and clearer the revelation of God will be. Furthermore, the capacity to receive theophanies depends upon the purity of the creature:

> Thus God will appear in his theophanies, that is, in the divine appearances, in which he will appear according to the degree of purity and virtue in each one. Theophanies, however, are all visible and invisible creatures, through which and in which God often appeared, is appearing, and will appear. Likewise, the powers of the purest souls and intellects [that is, angels] are theophanies, and God manifests himself to those who seek and love him.[66]

This should not lead one to believe, however, that the angels and the saints, as the highest and purest beings, are capable of understanding or fully revealing the Trinity. Both angels and men remain ignorant of the "interior" life of God and of their own essences in God: "For not even the angels know *what* they are, or *what* the Truth is: this is remote from every creature. But they only know *that* they are, and *that* the Truth superessentially is, and that all things proceed from it."[67] The deification of angels and men requires a greater theophany than just creation itself, a manifestation of God that reveals the deepest mystery of the Trinity. The Triune God must make himself known.

The Incarnation and the Angels

The question of the significance of the Incarnation for the angels offers an enlightening perspective regarding the Incarnation as effective theophany: does the Incarnation have any significance for the angels, beings of pure

64. *Peri.* V, 84, 2681–86.

65. *Peri.* I, 20, 509–10. "John thus consistently views creativity, in both God and man, as formative self-disclosure in word and symbol." Duclow, "Nothingness," 121.

66. *Comm.* I, xvii, 124, 83–95.

67. *Expo.* I, iii, 17, 606–10. On the of angels' and saints' ignorance see de Gandillac, "Anges et hommes," 397.

spirit? Since knowledge of God perfects the knower, the angels require deeper knowledge of the Trinity for their perfection. Yet how could the angels become initiated into the One who surpasses even their superior intellects?

Angels may only know of the Trinity if God renders himself accessible *as Trinity,* and this theophany of the immanent Trinity takes place through the Incarnation of the Son. The Word's descent into the flesh, as the supreme theophany, allows the angels to perceive the generation of the Son from the Father and the action of the Holy Spirit:

> Thus we believe and understand not in vain that the Incarnation of the Word of God was beneficial to angels no less than to man. For just as the Incarnation profited men for redemption and the restoration of their nature, so it gave the angels knowledge. Before the Word was made flesh, it was incomprehensible to every visible and invisible creature, that is, intellectual and rational, both angels and men, for it was separated and secret above all that is and is not. It is beyond everything that can be uttered or understood. But the incarnate Word, descending in a certain way by a miraculous, ineffable, and endlessly varied theophany, proceeded into the knowledge of angelic and human nature. The Unknown One, who is above all things, assumed from all things a nature in which he might be known, uniting the intelligible and sensible world in itself by an incomprehensible harmony. And the inaccessible light offered access to every intellectual and rational creature.[68]

The Incarnation becomes a theophany for both angels and men because it draws upon "all things," that is, from the material and the spiritual worlds. One may now *encounter* Christ, since the Word became visible both to the senses and the intellect through enfleshment.[69] This explains why the Word became man and not angel: the Word assumes man, who is the "workshop of the world" and the mediator of all creation.[70]

The Incarnation, therefore, helps the angels by giving them a comprehensible theophany of God as Trinity: the enfleshed Son also manifests the

68. *Peri.* V, 75, 2373–88.

69. This leads Hilary Mooney to speak of Eriugena's "theophanic Christology." In his *Commentarius in Sanctum Evangelium secundum Johannem,* "theophany is presented as encounter with Christ (*rapiuntur . . . obviam Christo*). This encounter is said to be granted to those who not only seek God (which could be a purely intellectual enterprise devoid of all attempts to live a moral life) but who in addition love God . . ." Mooney, *Theophany,* 172.

70. See *Hom.* XI, 256–58, 31–39.

Father and Spirit.[71] While creation itself reveals God, it does not manifest the deepest mysteries of the inner divine life. Only the Incarnation, demonstrating that God is One and Three, perfects the knowledge of the celestial ranks.

Purifying Humanity's Vision

What is a good for the angels is also a good for men. Men, too, receive their perfecting knowledge of the Trinity through the theophany of the Word made flesh. Eriugena sings of this great revelation in *Carmina* Eight:

> The mysteries of Christ are present no less in the heavens
> than on earth: and justly so, since God is One for all:
> There he perfected the angelic minds with light
> and offered them the shaded mysteries of his power.
> For no power was able to know in all purity
> the One whom the Father was hiding in his dark breast.
> But what a miracle! The Word now made flesh
> clearly reveals himself to all as man and God.[72]

For human beings, the Incarnation is a grace that reveals the truth of creation. Man receives "the perfect clarity of celestial grace which, by the incarnate Christ, most fully illuminates the world."[73] In Christ, one knows the Son and knows the unity of all that was made in him and through him. In fact, the theophany of the Incarnation takes place to elevate man's vision and lead him beyond the limited view of the senses to the comprehensive view of creation in God:

> The incarnate Word of God descended in order to lead human
> nature back to this vision [of all things in their primordial causes].
> He took on that previously fallen nature in order to recall it to the

71. Eriugena states that the Trinity becomes visible to men and angels in the Incarnation: "Thus the only-begotten Son 'spoke of God', that is, he manifested in himself—not in respect to his divinity, which is entirely invisible, but in respect to his humanity that he assumed—in order that he might reveal himself, his Father, and the Holy Spirit to men and angels." *Comm.* I, xviii, 128, 5–10. "For even the angels could not know their God in his nature, since God surpasses every intellect, because he is invisible and unknown. But when the Word became incarnate, they knew their God, as the Son of God, and in him and through him they knew the entire Trinity, which is separate from all creatures." *Comm.* I, xviii, 116, 17–22.

72. *Carm.* VIII, 86, 43–50.

73. *Comm.* IV, ii, 290, 58–61.

original state. He healed the wounds of its crimes, extinguished the shadows of false fantasies, opened the eyes of the mind, and revealed himself in all those things to those who are worthy of such a vision.[74]

The Incarnation heals the distorted vision of humanity, leading all from the sensible revelation of the flesh to the unifying vision of the divinity.[75]

Purifying Humanity's Worship

The theophany that is the Incarnation also leads man into authentic worship, drawing him away from the material idols of creation and into true spiritual adoration. In his commentary on Jesus's encounter with the Samaritan woman at the well (John 4:19–24), Eriugena pauses to reflect on the words: "The hour has come, even now, when the true adorers will adore the Father in Spirit and in truth" (John 4:23). Eriugena imagines Jesus's own explanation of the verse: "Before I came, no one was able to adore the Father in spirit and truth, except for the Patriarchs and Prophets, to whom my presence in the flesh was revealed through the Spirit before I came into the world."[76] The Patriarchs and Prophets required an accessible, comprehensible vision of the Word-made-flesh in order to approach God—even before the Incarnation took place historically! The human intellect, through knowing Jesus, is therefore "cleansed first through faith, illuminated through knowledge, and perfected through deification on the mount of *theologia.*"[77]

Thus the knowledge of the Word incarnate is but a first step, a way of leaving the material behind and rising up to a more profound union with God. One cannot rest with Christ on earth, but must also follow him in the ascension. Again, commenting on the story of the woman at the well, Eriugena stops to ponder the verse: "The woman left her jug behind" (John

74. *Peri.* III, 92, 2678–82.

75. "That incomprehensible light of the Father was inaccessible to us before the light that was generated from him—Christ—was incarnate and became man. Since, however, he became human and was made in our nature, we have access to the invisible Father. For when we understand the humanity of Christ, we know perfectly—to the extent that we are allowed to know—the hidden divinity of the Son, his Father, and the Spirit of both." *Expo.* I, i, 7, 234–40.

76. *Comm.* IV, vii, 316, 46–49.

77. *Comm.* IV, vii, 316–18, 49–54.

4:28). He states that "after the Church or human nature knows the presence of the divine substance [person] in the flesh, it leaves behind its jug, that is, it abandons its carnal habits, it leaves behind the water and the zeal for carnal knowledge."[78] The theophany of the incarnate Word reveals God in order that man might enter more deeply into the mystery.

The Expression of God's Love and Mercy toward Man

The most important reason for the Incarnation is God's love. Eriugena does not reduce the descent of the Word to a divine "obligation" for the sake of jump-starting the movement of creation toward union. Instead, he highlights the truth that Christ's "charity and clemency embrace the entire human race. . . . He loved all men equally, when he handed himself over for all."[79] The true impetus behind the merciful divine *kenosis* is the desire to fill the gap left in creation through man's selfishness. Christ came to restore love to nature: "This is the most widely embracing law of nature, which [Christ] fulfilled in himself, suffering death for all. Indeed the law of nature is the common love of all men without an exception of persons. This law was most perfectly fulfilled in Christ, and it proceeded from the Father, 'who did not spare his own Son, but for our sake handed him over for all' (Rom 8:32)."[80] Even the angels marvel at Christ's "human, that is, gentle goodness toward the salvation of human kind."[81]

Love and mercy shaped God's plan for fallen humanity "from the beginning." Eriugena imagines God's response to man's expulsion from paradise:

> Now I see man expelled from paradise and rendered wretched, when once he was good; needy, when once he was rich; temporal, when once he was eternal; mortal, when once he had life; foolish, when once he was wise; an animal, when once he was spiritual; earthly, when once he was heavenly; grown old, when once he was young; sad, when once he was joyful; lost, when once he was safe; prodigal, when once he was a prudent son; he wandered away from the flock of heavenly powers—I mourn for him![82]

78. *Comm.* IV, viii, 322, 39–42.
79. *Peri.* V, 200, 6494–98.
80. *Peri.* V, 200, 6500–6503.
81. *Expo.* VII, iii, 109, 690–94.
82. *Peri.* V, 5, 73–83; 91–94.

God's mercy leads to the descent of the Word, who is the just judge and savior of man.[83] God does not leave his beloved image in misery, but comes to seek the lamb that had wandered from the flock of the heavenly powers.

Conclusions

Eriugena offers various reasons for the Word's descent into the causes: the recreation of the cosmos; the restoration of human nature; the salvation of the effects; the redemption of man and the destruction of sin; the revelation through an effective theophany; and an expression of God's love and mercy. In formulating these reasons, Eriugena proves himself to be a faithful and creative reader of the Scriptures and tradition.

Yet one reason remains to be explored: the resurrection of Jesus and the deification of man. God became man, that man might become God. The next two chapters will explore this central theme in Eriugena's work from the perspective of a "participatory" Christology: the Incarnation calls for a free response from man to the gift of divine grace—a grace that will make all things one in God.

---

83. "For what greater justice is there than that the Creator recall the creature, which he had made in his own image, and remakes him similar to himself; what greater judgment is there than that he punish in the creature what he did not make, and frees what he made." *Expo.* VII, iii, 110, 699–703.

4

The Foundations
of Participatory Christology

THE RESTORATION AND DEIFICATION OF man could not take place without
the incarnate Word: man is transformed through his participation in the
Word-made-flesh. Certainly the unification of natures in Christ effects the
transformation of creation, but this does not preclude man's free application of his natural faculties in cooperation with grace. Man must mystically
incorporate the path of Jesus into his own life, making a *transitus* through
the mysteries of the Incarnation and entering into divine union. This chapter summarizes the grounds of each person's free participation in Christ.

Transformation in Christ

The Objective Pole: The Miraculous Exchange

Without the full sweep of the Incarnation—the birth, life, death, resurrection, and ascension—the salvation and deification of man could never take
place. Eriugena justifies this position, in part, on the model of the "miraculous exchange" (*admirabile commercium*): God became man in order that
man might become God. This represents "the objective pole" of deification,
since man's elevation depends entirely upon the giftedness of the Incarnation that reforms creation:

What mind, what power, what created wisdom from on high
could say something of the descent of the Word into the flesh,
and know of the sublime steps of the flesh into the Word!
As the eternal God-made-flesh descended into the depths,
so the flesh made truly God weightlessly (*levis*) flies into the
heights.[1]

The unification of natures in the person of Jesus Christ results in the descent of the Word into the flesh and the ascent of the flesh into God: "If the Son of God was made man—and there is not doubt about this among those who receive Him!—what is so surprising if man, believing in the Son of God, will be a son of God? For this reason indeed, the Word descended into the flesh, in order that the flesh—that is, man—by believing in Him, might ascend into the Word through the flesh."[2] In rising from the dead and ascending to the right hand of the Father, the Son transforms all of human nature and bears it into the heart of the divine mystery.

For this reason, Eriugena emphasizes the authenticity of Christ's resurrected body and the elevation of that body to divine unity. There exists a continuity between the material body of Jesus and his resurrected, spiritual body that returned to the paradise of human nature. What takes place in Christ's resurrection cannot be a complete break from his earthly life, but a transformation and elevation. It is a movement from the fragmentation of material existence to the unity in spirit; then from unity in spirit to intimacy in God: "In such a [spiritual] body we believe Christ appeared to his disciples after the resurrection, not because it was something different from the body born of the Virgin, suspended on the cross, and brought back from the dead. It was, rather, that the same body changed from mortal into immortal, from animal into spiritual, from earthly into celestial."[3] The continuity of the Word's genuine body shows that "all things are from Him and to Him all things return: for He is the Beginning and the End."[4]

The unification with God, therefore, will only take place through the miraculous restoration of natures in the person of Christ: "If God the Word had not been made flesh, and had not dwelt among men, and had not

1. *Carm.* XXV, 118, 67–71.
2. *Hom.* XXI, 306, 20–24.
3. *Peri.* V, 186, 6054–59.
4. *Peri.* V, 48, 1503–4.

received the fullness of human nature, in which he suffered and rose, there would be no resurrection from the dead."[5]

The Subjective Pole: Christ as Mediator and Pattern

The deification of man in Christ, however, also requires the free appropriation of the *life* of the incarnate Word. The restoration and unification of man with God does not take place through the hypostatic union alone, as if it were a chemical reaction. The pattern of the Incarnation—the ascent of Word—designates the path for humanity's willing participation in salvation and deification: *how* Jesus lived is as important as *what* Jesus was. This represents the "subjective pole" for the believer, since it demands a personal and mystical imitation of the Word-made-flesh.[6] The way of Christ—his life, his passion, his resurrection, his ascension—establishes a manner of existence for humanity.

Eriugena adopts the series of mediations formulated by Maximus the Confessor in order to show how the pattern of ascent established by the incarnate Word restores and elevates creation. Man, "the workshop of the world," originally received the mission to mediate between the distinctions of: 1) male and female; 2) paradise and the habitable earth; 3) heaven and the earth; 4) the intelligible and the sensible; and 5) the uncreated and created.[7] In short, man was meant to unify the diversity of creation in himself as the mediator, to the point that his own deification in God's grace would bear all things to God. Yet, as we have already seen, he failed in his mission on account of the fall and remained closed to the grace required for the union of created and uncreated. Man became the cause of fragmentation, not the source of unity.

Christ, however, came to perform these mediations *as man* through his life, death, resurrection, and ascension, thereby allowing all of humanity to follow his path: "And our Lord and savior Jesus Christ fulfilled all of these [mediations] in himself by rising from the dead, and gave an example

---

5. *Peri.* V, 57, 1788–91.

6. Bernard McGinn focuses upon the subjective *imitatio Christi* that occurs through an ascent through levels of knowledge. Yet, as we shall see, Eriugena's *imitatio* also involves a performative, ethical imitation that involves the active growth in the virtues. See McGinn, "Mysticus," 252.

7. For these divisions in Maximus see *Peri.* II, 18–19, 378–90; *Peri.* V, 48–49, 1507–26. Also see Maximus, *Ambigua* XLI, 1305C ff; Thunberg, *Microcosm*, 373–425; Studer, "Soteriologie," 242–43.

of all the things that will take place in the future."[8] The descent and ascent of the Word completes the essential unifications that man had abandoned and draws all to the Father. Now man himself may assume the same path of restoration and deification, since the Word established the pattern in his own life.[9]

Man must mystically follow this ascent established in Christ through both faith and action. The evangelist John stands out as a prime example of one who ascended with Christ, becoming himself, for a time, a deified witness to sublime mysteries: "Therefore John was not a man, but more than a man, when he rose beyond himself and all things which exist. Carried by the ineffable power of wisdom and by the purest keenness of mind, he entered into those things which are above all things, that is, the secrets of one essence in three substances [persons] and of three substances in one essence."[10] Man, like John, must cultivate wisdom and purity of mind in order to follow the path of Jesus into the secret folds of divine union.

At first, it may appear that one enters into the pattern of Christ's ascent as an unwilling passenger, borne upwards through the elevated human nature of Christ (the objective pole). Yet, as we shall see, one must become "worthy" to participate in the Truth. Eriugena, while discussing the second division of creation (paradise and the inhabitable earth), notes that "it is not by mass or space that paradise is distinguished from the inhabitable globe of the earth, but by the diversity in ways of living (*conversatio*) and the difference in beatitude."[11] Certainly this transformation of the person requires grace; but it also involves an ascetical program that follows Christ's ascent through a manner of living. The next section examines how one may set out on the way established by Jesus Christ.

8. *Peri.* V, 49, 1546–48.

9 "But, if He alone ascended, what hope is there for those for whom he descended? Indeed there is a great and inexplicable hope, since all, who ascended in him, now *through faith and hope*, but in the end truly by sight in reality, just as John said in his letter: 'We know that we are sons of God. What we will be has not yet appeared. Since, however, he appeared, we will be similar to him. For we will see him as he is' (1 John 3:2). He alone descended, and he alone ascended, because he alone is God with all his members—the only Son of God. For in him all those who believe in him are one. For one is Christ, the body with his members, who ascends to the Father." *Comm.* III, v, 224, 27–37.

10 *Hom.* V, 220–24, 1–17. John enters into the mystery of the Trinity itself: "Thus the blessed theologian John flies above not only those things which can be understood or expressed, but also into those things which surpass every intellect and transcend all signification . . . ." *Hom.* I, 206–8, 13–21.

11. *Peri.* II, 19, 400–402.

The Grounds for Participation in the Incarnation

"Given," "Gift," "Well-being," and "Non-being"

The deification of man takes place within the polarity of natural "givens" (*dationes*) and divinely bestowed "gifts" (*donationes*). The perfection and elevation of the creature, therefore, emerges within both nature (the "given") and grace (the "gift"):

> The difference between givens (*dationes*) and gifts (*donationes*) is as follows: The givens are and are said to be appropriately the distributions by which every nature subsists, while gifts truly are distributions of grace by which every subsisting nature is adorned. Therefore, nature is a given (*datio*), grace is something gifted (*donatio*). Indeed every perfect creature is constituted by nature and grace. Therefore, it is established that every essence (*essentia*) is called a given, every virtue (*virtus*) is called a gift. So the theologian says: "Every given (*datum*) is the best and every perfect gift (*donum*) has descended from above, from the Father of lights (James 1:17)."[12]

The polarity between "given" and "gift" in man, in fact, reflects Eriugena's appropriation of a fundamental teaching of Maximus the Confessor. Maximus distinguished the "being" of man's nature (τὸ εἶναι, corresponding with Eriugena's "given") from the "eternal-being" in God (τὸ ἀεὶ εἶναι, corresponding with Eriugena's "gift").[13] Man depends entirely upon God for these poles of his existence: no man can give himself being, no man can raise himself up to eternal being. Man's *given* nature sets the parameters within which his essence unfolds; the divine *gifts* (graces) allow man to reach the transcendent end—eternal divine union—for which his essence was created.

This schema, as Eriugena presents it, appears to preclude an openness to autonomy or self-realization: one receives a *given* nature that in turn acquires the adornments of divine *gifts* that elevate it to a supernatural end. This seems to confirm that Eriugena accepts an *exitus-reditus* vision that ignores the individual person in favor of a grand cosmic process: secret

---

12. *Peri.* III, 20, 542–51. Also see *Expo.* I, i, 1–2, 30–39: "Everything that exists shares in the divine goodness in two modes, the first of which is seen in the condition of nature, the second in the distribution of grace."

13. See Maximus, *Ambigua* X, 116B; Renczes, *Agir*, 182–85.

channels of grace may unite all things, but that union has no room for autonomous creatures.

Yet Eriugena also adopts a third element from Maximus that lies between the given (the being of nature) and gift (the grace of eternal-being), namely, "well-being" (τὸ εὖ εἶναι), which represents the sphere of human freedom and autonomy. The state of "eternal-being" emerges from the manner in which the creature shapes his "well-being" in this life, that is, through the growth in virtues and contemplation. Thus Eriugena writes, "nature will not be equally blessed for all, but the nature in all will be free of death and misery. For 'to be and to live' [*datio*] and 'to be eternally' [*donatio*] will be common to all, both good and evil; but 'being well' and 'being blessed' will be the particular property of those alone who are perfect in action and in knowledge."[14]

Eriugena develops Maximus's thought further by stating that the quality of "well-being," in effect, increases or decreases man's being. When a creature deviates from its true nature, perverting its mind and will, it ceases truly "to be," that is, it becomes less itself.[15] A creature's authenticity, therefore, requires cooperation between free will and grace in order to exist properly and blessedly according to its essence:

> Truly, between "being" and "eternal-being" stands a certain mediator that is called "well-being," without which the extremes themselves (that is, "being" and "eternal-being") do not truly exist—although they do exist!—and they are not said genuinely "to be." If "well-being" should be taken away, "to be" is not truly said "to be," nor is "to be forever" truly said "to be forever." For that thing truly is and always is, which subsists well and blessedly. This intervening mediator (that is, "well-being") is a gift of divine goodness, along with the free and good motion of the intellectual and rational creature's will. Thus "well-being" is achieved through two things: by free will and by divine gift, which the Holy Scriptures call grace.[16]

Eriugena asserts, therefore, that the creature's deviation from its essence drags it into "non-being" and unintelligibility, while only "well-being" constitutes the rational and intellectual being as it truly *is*. Furthermore, proper "well-being" requires the effective application of the will toward the

14. *Peri.* V, 13, 333–38.
15. On the modes of being and non–being see *Peri.* I, 4–8, 45–153.
16. *Peri.* V, 63, 2008–18.

Good, along with the aid of supernatural grace. In short, the manner in which *what* something is (given/gift, being/eternal-being) emerges from *how* something is (well-being/non-being).

Man, therefore, possesses a dynamism through the exercise of free will and the reception of divinely bestowed graces,[17] which allow an essence to go beyond its natural powers to acquire a divinely intended fulfillment. As will be shown through the example of the resurrection, Eriugena accepts the paradoxical position that an essence may possess the potential for an end that may only be achieved through divine aid or grace. A given nature requires the adornment of supernatural gifts: "Nature is a given (*datum*), grace truly is a gift (*donum*). Nature brings existing things out of non-existing things; the gift brings certain existing things beyond all existing things into God himself."[18]

Participation

Eriugena develops these concepts of "given" and "gift" within a discussion of the theme of participation. The givens and gifts of created natures come from God, but emerge through a network of dynamic participations in a divinely ordered cosmos. He notes that the Greek terms for participation, μετοχή and μετουσία, both have the prefix μετα, that is, "after": a participant "has after" (μετοχή), or is an "after essence" or "second essence" (μετουσία), since it participates in the One that gives it being.[19] Every creature receives its essence from and participates in the source of all being:

> Thus one may easily understand that participation is nothing else but the derivation from a superior essence of the second essence after it, and the distribution from that which first has being to the second essence. We can demonstrate this from examples from nature. Indeed, the whole river flows principally from the source and through its channel the water, which comes forth in the source, is dispersed into whatever distance it extends. It is diffused always without any intermission. Thus divine Goodness and Essence and Life and Wisdom and all things that are in the Source of all things

17. In fact, free will applies to the exercise of one's given nature; free will cannot create grace. "One must understand that the free will is considered regarding the givens of nature, not the gifts of grace." *Expo.* XV, iii, 196, 318–20.

18. *Peri.* V, 64, 2062–65.

19. On the sources of these terms see Proclus, *Institutio,* Prop. i–iii, 2–5; Dionysius, *De celesti hierarchia* VIII, ii, 34, 1–16; Lilla, *Dionigi l'Areopagita,* 179.

flow first into the primordial causes and cause them to be, then through the primordial causes they flow down into their effects in an ineffable way through the orders of the universe appropriate to them, always from the highest to the lowest streams. And again they return to their font through the most secret channels of nature by a most hidden passage.[20]

This passage portrays the cosmos as a flowing forth from God and a return to God, in which being and grace continuously unite the whole. Each existent, in fact, participates in God in the manner appropriate to it, receiving being, goodness, and life. Man, above all, can never be considered apart from this sharing in the divine, since his being, well-being, and eternal-being cannot be sustained and realized apart from the Creator.[21]

In the fall, man fruitlessly attempted to divorce himself from participation in God, deceived by the desire to define his own nature and all those natures in him. This, of course, was a foolish exercise: man can never exist apart from God. Yet he ceased looking toward the image in which he was made and refused to cooperate with his state of dependence. The way of the flesh continues this impossible rebellion against the Creator and Sustainer of Being.

The healing of man, therefore, requires a return to free cooperation with the state of participation. Eriugena teaches that man's participation in God comes specifically through sharing in Christ. In his discussion of the incarnate Word as the "All-Tree" in paradise, he explains how man must freely share in Christ and how the abandonment of Christ led to the fall:

For it [the All-Tree, the incarnate Word] alone is the substantial Good. Other things, which are said to be good, are not good in themselves, but are good by participation in it. [The All-Tree] is the truly existing Good in itself. It is every good, goodness, fount and origin of every good and goodness, cause and beginning, end and perfection, motion and rest, middle and extreme, environment and place. Its fruit is eternal life. Its food is joy and happiness and ineffable delights. . . . But our first parents did not want to take their food from there, preferring the death-dealing fruit of

20. *Peri.* III, 21, 557–70.

21. "Thus, when we hear that God makes all things, we must understand nothing else than that God is in all things, that is, he is the essence of all things. For he alone 'is' through himself, and everything which is said truly 'to be' in those things that are, is God alone. For none of those things that are, truly 'is' through itself. But whatever is truly understood [to be] in it, it receives by participation in the One who alone truly 'is' through himself." *Peri.* I, 104, 3258–64.

the forbidden tree. Not only they, but also the entire race produced from them, were expelled from the dignity of their nature by the most just divine judgment and condemned to death.[22]

The passage implies that man's selfish turn at the dawn of creation came from a rejection of Jesus, the *incarnate* Word and All-Tree, who both created and sustains humanity. In effect, man, from the moment of his creation, saw his nature and all of creation expressed and defined by the incarnate Word—and rejected him. Instead, man sought to define himself and to see creation only in reference to himself. The refusal to participate in the life of Jesus—to be shaped by the Christ-form—led to death and decay; the restoration to life, therefore, demands an imitation of the Word-made-flesh

Asceticism and Individual Formation

The Three Stages of the Spiritual Life

Scholars accuse Eriugena of failing to develop an ascetic or spiritual program for humanity.[23] He seems to ignore the fruits of his esteemed mentors—Augustine, Gregory of Nyssa, Maximus the Confessor—in favor of an impersonal, Neoplatonic "process" that raises creation to divine union. Is this accusation fair?

In fact, Eriugena's writings do outline a spiritual program that unfolds within the scope of "well-being." *Carmina* Twenty-Four, for instance, offers a three-step ladder that finds its primary inspiration in the works of Evagrius Ponticus[24] and Maximus the Confessor:[25] *praktike* (the active or acetic stage), *physike* (natural contemplation), and *theologia* (mystical contemplation):

> Thus *praktike* shines as the bright teacher of morals,
> the vigilant and worthy guardian of virtues.
> Thus *physike* examines the hidden causes of things,
> and simultaneously separates and unites what it finds.
> Thus *theologia*—the most beautiful of all, she bears the palm!—
> denies simultaneously what is and what is not.[26]

22. *Peri.* IV, 116–17, 3495–3502; 3509–13.

23. For example see Colish, "Christology," 138.

24. See Evagrius, *Praktikos* I, 498, 1–2. Also see Driscoll, *Steps*, 11–37.

25. For instance, see Maximus, *Ambigua* VII, 1081D; *Ambigua* X, 1109A.

26. *Carm.* XXIV, 114, 15–20. This poem is an encomium to Maximus the Confessor.

Maximus the Confessor, who borrowed these stages from Evagrius, states that *praktike* represents "the rational soul's freedom from passion. Through asceticism the soul has entirely thrown off the stings of sin."[27] In *physike* the mind arrives "at the contemplation of visible things and seeks either their natural reasons, or the things symbolized through them, or it seeks the cause itself of these things."[28] In this stage man escapes the deceptions of sensory experience and comes to see the causes in God through the Book of Nature. Finally, *theologia* is the mystical experience of God, in which God is perceived "without knowledge, by indemonstrable initiations into the mysteries; or, to say it more properly, he has the word of faith known apart from concepts, over which no created thing may be placed."[29]

Eriugena generally accepts these basic definitions. Yet he will also develop them in creative ways within his own thought, in some cases even linking them to the definitions of the Dionysian stages of ascent: purgation, illumination, and perfection.[30]

Praktike

> Thus *praktike* shines as the bright teacher of morals
> the vigilant and worthy guardian of virtues.

To make the *transitus* from the flesh to the Word, one must eliminate the vices and grow in the splendor of the virtues. St. Paul commands, "You must mortify your members which are upon the earth" (Col 3:5). Eriugena believes this verse to mean: "Mortify the members of vice—for they are yours, since they were made from your disobedience, and not from God—from which you build a universal body of vice on the earth, that is, on the

---

One, can, however find some influences in Eriugena's reading of Augustine, particularly in the identification of *theologia* as wisdom. See Madec, "*Theologia*," 117–21.

27. Maximus, *Capita theologica* I, xxvii, 1098C.

28. Maximus, *Capita de caritate* I, xcviii, 88.

29. Maximus, *Thalassium* XXV, 161, 54–61.

30. See *Expo.* X, iii, 156, 179–87. Eriugena demonstrates the progression of virtues in each stage: "Those wise in theology call the first virtues, which are in both the human and celestial mind, theological; the middle virtues, natural; the last virtues, moral. The first are particularly called primary because they are around God; but the middle are so-called because they are around created nature; the last are not mistakenly designated because they are around morals, which follow nature and fulfill the duties of their powers." *Expo.* X, iii, 157, 199–205.

solidity of the nature created by God, lest you be polluted by them further." By stripping away the elements of fallen nature, one may construct "members of justice, which are the virtues, in place of the destructive members of vice."[31]

Again, drawing upon Pauline images, he stresses the need to strip away "the outer man" (2 Cor 4:16) and reform one's life. This demands a separation from the blandishments and deceptions of the flesh in favor of the adornments of virtue:

> For whoever lives perfectly must not only spurn, but also, as far as possible, break to pieces and destroy completely his body and the life by which it is administered; and all the corporeal senses, along with the things he perceives through them; and all the irrational motions which he feels in himself with the memory of all mutable things. He does this lest in any way they dominate in him, for he desires to be dead to them and they to him. He renews himself truly, to the degree that he is a participant in the celestial essence "day by day," that is, ascending from virtue to virtue through the aid of divine grace, which moves, cooperates, leads, and perfects. And, indeed, that nature, which man shares with animals, is called flesh; and truly that nature by which he is a participant in the divine essence is mind, soul, or intellect.[32]

This stripping of the outer man should be interpreted neither as a rejection of creation nor as a rejection of the human body itself. Rather, Eriugena calls for a separation from the flesh—the corrupted elements that emerged from sin—in order that one may approach God.[33] One must transcend the instability of fallen existence through active reform and the recovery of the state of the spirit.[34] Cooperating with grace, man enters the struggle to grow in the virtues, which restore the harmony of his nature.[35]

31. *Peri.* IV, 9–10, 206–12.

32. *Peri.* IV, 18, 460–71.

33. "The action of the divine commandments comes first in the ascent of the virtues, through which both the rational and intellectual creatures' interior eye of the mind is cleansed in order that one—free and absolved from every vain phantasy and the fog of the vices—may sustain the intimate rays of the highest Good that is diffused through all things." *Expo.* III, i, 56, 29–34.

34. *Praktike* "investigates the virtues, by which the vices are supplanted and eradicated from within." *Peri.* III, 124, 3586–3587.

35. "Such is the difference between virtues and vices, because vices are different from one another and conflict with one another; but virtues are similar to one another, like a smooth, well-rounded wheel. Thus one virtue generally seems to be all virtues and all

It is, in the end, a dying to self and the world in order to see all things in God.[36] In commenting on the Beatitude, "Blessed are the meek, since they will possess the earth" (Matt 5:5), Eriugena teaches:

> For it is necessary that those who are meek in evil—that is, having no part in any evil—be bold in the good—that is, in the serious and diligent guarding of the virtues. They must be moved by their zeal for them and by their laudable anger [against vice]. They never cease to fight against all the vices with an ever-vigilant mind, lest the vices prevail. They rest in the peace of the virtues that they guard.[37]

Praktike, however, requires more than just the exercise of human will and discipline for growth in the virtues. Eriugena highlights the necessity of baptism for new life in the Spirit: "For when each one of the faithful experiences the sacrament of baptism, what else is taking place there, if not the conception and birth of the Word of God in their hearts from the Holy Spirit and through the Holy Spirit? Thus daily Christ is conceived, born, and nourished in the womb of faith, as in the womb of a most chaste mother."[38] Baptism is the sacrament that liberates one from original sin and initiates the healing through action and contemplation: "[Baptism] frees us from the crime of sin and raises us to the grace of divine filiation, in order that, when the crime is removed, the wounds of our crimes may begin to be healed. For as long as the crime remains in the wound, like an arrow, it is not possible to heal any wound; however when it is taken out, a place for spiritual medicine is opened."[39] Therefore, *praktike* requires both the will and the grace that comes from the saving waters of the sacrament.[40]

The grace of baptism, in turn, forms one for the way of faith in Christ, the only path toward divine union. "Indeed, the first illumination of the

---

seem to be one, though natural differences are united to their harmony." *Expo.* XV, iv, 202, 543–47. On the unity of the virtues see Gregorius Nyssenus, *De beatitudinibus* IV, 118, 19–20; Radde-Gallwitz, *Transformation*, 207–12.

36. *Peri.* V, 56, 1755–59.

37. *Expo.* II, iv, 41, 775–82.

38. *Peri.* II, 119, 2975–80.

39. *Comm.* I, xxxiii, 192–94, 46–51. Also see *Expo.* VIII, ii, 129, 398–404.

40. Eriugena highlights the manner in which the sign of baptism cleanses the exterior body, but its effect is interior and salvific. "Since man is comprised of a visible body and an invisible soul, it is necessary that a sacrament be visible for the purification of the visible body, just as it is necessary that it be invisible as the doctrine of the faith for the sanctification of the invisible soul." *Comm.* III, ii, 210, 30–34.

rational soul that is returning to its creator is the gift of faith, which is given and symbolized by the sacrament of baptism."[41] Faith is the essential, divinely bestowed virtue for the follower of Christ: "For through no other way does the Lord enter the hearts of men except through faith, which is the way of the Lord."[42] The way of faith sustains one's liberation from original sin and "makes straight" the journey into God.[43] It is not, however, the end or goal, for it is only that which leads to the higher gift: the understanding of the Lord in contemplation.[44]

Therefore, the first stage of the spiritual life involves the exercise of the given nature and the reception of the gift of grace: the liberation of baptism and the exercise of virtues. In this way one assumes Peter's manner of following Jesus—action, *praktike*—and continues on to John's form of imitating Christ—*physike, theologike*:

> Therefore, Peter, that is, the action of the virtues, *observes the Son of God, surrounded by the flesh* in a miraculous and ineffable way, *through the virtue of faith and action.* But John, that is, the highest contemplation of virtue, *sees* the Word of God in an absolute sense, through himself, as the Word was before he had put on the flesh and was still infinite in his origin, that is, in his Father. Peter, led by divine revelation, sees at the same time eternal and temporal things in Christ. John brings the eternal things alone of Christ into the knowledge of faithful souls.[45]

Eriugena links *praktike* to the person of Christ. One cannot grow in virtue and grace without considering "the principles for the Incarnation of the Word." This means embracing "the entire moral philosophy concerning the virtues of the soul and the flesh of Christ."[46] By observing Christ in the flesh, one sees the principles of living the active Christian life.

41. *Expo.* II, v, 45, 943–46.

42. *Comm.* I, xxviii, 144, 7–9.

43. *Comm.* III, xii, 276, 65–66.

44. "'To those who believe in his name' (John 1:12), that is, to those who believe that they will receive knowledge of Him and understanding through faith in this life, and through vision in the next." *Comm.* I, xxi, 98, 16–18.

45. *Hom.* III, 216, 28–36.

46. *Comm.* I, xxxii, 184, 49–52.

Physike

> Thus *physike* examines the hidden causes of things,
> and simultaneously separates (*segregat*) and unites (*unificat*) what
> it finds.

Natural contemplation is *scientia*, a genuine knowledge of things as theophanies of God.[47] At this stage, purged of the cloud of vices, one "desires by a natural motion to see all things that are after God, and everything that one can perceive with the power of the intellect is given to the praise of the Creator."[48] It requires a shift in perspective, from the divisive vision of the fall to the unifying vision in God.

Eriugena equates *physike*, in part, with philosophy and the art of dialectic. Philosophy is not simply an intellectual exercise, but rather it is a spiritual path that heals the perception of reality. Man's contemplation of things applies the operations of division and resolution,[49] which mirror the divine *exitus-reditus* schema: after seeing the division and multiplication of things (the *exitus*), dialectic applies the rules of synthesis to see things in their unity (the *reditus*).[50] Philosophy and its dialectical operations heal the human mind, which destroyed creation's unity through its selfish turn:[51] *Nemo intrat in caelum nisi per philosophiam.*[52]

In the verse from Eriugena's poem cited above, one can see the influence of dialectic upon his understanding of natural contemplation. *Physike* calls for the separation and unification of the hidden causes of things: it is the healing of the human mind.[53] One must observe the Book of

47. ". . . the *physica theoria* is a deciphering of the theophanies present in the sensible world. The 'physical,' that is scientific, interpretation of the world must be outgrown in order for us to pass in the direction of theophanies of a higher order, that is, towards understanding reality in the light of its immutable causes." Kijewska, "Theology," 179–80.

48. *Expo.* III, i, 56, 33–36.

49. *Diairetike* and *analysis.* See *Expo.* VII, ii, 106–7, 580–87; *Peri.* II, 5, 49–62.

50. *Peri.* V, 14, 364–70. Also see d'Onofrio, *Vera Philosophia*, 162–68; Eristmann, "Logic," 207.

51. "Dialectical process is not for Eriugena, as it had been for Aristotle, a process of abstraction, still less some kind of postmodern process of construction, but a real participation by the human mind in the cosmic workings of the Logos . . ." Kavanagh, "Dialectic," 35. Also see Bisogno, *Metodo*, 346–47; Moran, *Philosophy*, 124.

52. *Annotationes* LVII, xv, 64, 20.

53. Thus *physike* "investigates the reasons of natures, either in the causes or in the effects." *Peri.* III, 124, 3582–94.

Nature in order to find its hidden principles, and then perform the exercises of division and analysis in order to return to the Source of unity.[54] Again, for Eriugena, this is not an esoteric cognitive performance, but rather a spiritual reunification of things through the proper exercise of the human intellect in contemplation. In effect, it is the healing of the second motion of the soul—reason or power (λόγος-δύναμις; *ratio-virtus*)—that knows that "God is the cause of all things that exist, and that the primordial causes of all things are created by him and in him eternally."[55]

Natural contemplation cannot, however, divorce itself from Christ. Above all, it is the contemplation of "the rational soul that Christ received."[56] While *praktike* learns the virtues through contemplation of the flesh of Christ, *physike* goes deeper and comes to see that the soul of Christ transforms his flesh. Man learns that the soul must elevate and transform the body through a shift in vision in order that it might enter into the unity of the resurrection.[57]

Theologia

> Thus *theologia*—the most beautiful of all, it bears the palm!—
> denies simultaneously what is and what is not.

Mystical contemplation is a gift, a flight into the divine intimacy.[58] When Eriugena describes this experience as "what one must piously think regarding the one cause of all things, which is God," he may sound like an indifferent scholar pondering a recondite problem.[59] In fact, for the Irishman, this stage represents the peak of all human experience, the sphere of the "aether and the fiery ardor of the heavenly empyrean—the highest contemplation of divine nature."[60] *Theologia* "considers only the divine things which surpass every intellect, with the gnostic virtue of the most burn-

---

54. Eriugena repeats Maximus the Confessor's teaching that nature reveals the Word through proper contemplation. See *Comm.* I, xxix, 154–56, 52–68.

55. *Peri.* II, 69, 1584–85. Also see Roques, *Libres*, 136–37.

56. *Comm.* I, xxxii, 184, 56–57.

57. See *Comm.* I, xxxii, 184–86, 58–67.

58. In this contemplation one ascends "into God himself, to whom he will be similar and in whom he will wordlessly rest." *Expo.* III, i, 57, 39–40.

59. *Peri.* III, 124, 3582–94.

60. *Hom.* XIV, 270–72, 14–17.

ing charity."[61] Its object is the "intellect of Christ," the incarnate Word in his perfect unity with God. The one who receives this gift leaves all things behind to share in the divine infinitude.[62]

Eriugena begins his homily on the Prologue of John's Gospel with a powerful depiction of the Evangelist's flight into mystical contemplation—a depiction so compelling and vivid that it may come from the Irishman's own experience:

> The voice of the spiritual eagle strikes the ears of the Church! The exterior sense receives the sound coming in; the interior spirit penetrates the waiting intellect. It is the voice of a high-flying eagle—not of a bird flying over corporeal air or the aether or the environment of all sensible things, but of the one transcending all things that are and are not, with the swift wings of intimate *theologia*, with the view of the supreme and clearest contemplation. . . . Thus the blessed theologian John soars above not only things that can be understood or expressed, but also into those things which surpass every intellect and surpass all meaning. He is borne up beyond all things, by an ineffable flight of the mind, into the secrets of the One Principle of all things. He discerns purely the incomprehensible and united superessentiality, and the distinct supersubtantiality of the Principle and of the Word, that is, of the Father and the Son. And so he says at the beginning of his Gospel, *In the beginning there was the Word* (John 1:10).[63]

All persons should hunger for this flight into the Word: the experience of the intimate mysteries of God.

Taking on the Form of Christ

Eriugena reveals the importance of asceticism and contemplation—*praktike, physike,* and *theologia*—in the return and deification: while the entrance into divine union takes place through both the given of nature and the grace of Christ—given and gift, being and eternal-being—the *state* of this union with God depends upon the exercise of freedom in the sphere of well-being.[64] Furthermore, as we have seen, all of these stages include the

61. *Expo.* II, v, 46, 962–65.

62. *Comm.* I, xxxii, 186–88, 68–75.

63. *Hom.* XV, 201–8, 1–8; 13–21.

64. "None of us is led back unwillingly, lest the natural glory of the divine image, which was given to us fully with the liberty of free will, come to naught. The election,

appropriation of the incarnate Word: Jesus's flesh, soul, and intellect. The spiritual life, therefore, requires taking on the form of Christ.

The manner in which one passes through the spiritual stages shapes one's personal participation in God. Eriugena speaks of the importance of merit and free choices through the image of the Father's house having many rooms (John 14:2):

> Thus it is understood that all men are participants in one and the same nature, which was redeemed in Christ and liberated from all servitude, under which it still groans and is saddened. Those who subsist in that nature are one. Yet the qualities and quantities of their merits—that is, the differences between their good and evil acts, by which each one either lived well in this life through the aid of God's grace, or lived evilly in this life, having been justly abandoned by God—differ greatly and in infinitely varied ways. All these things, however, are ordered and understood in that one, all-embracing house, in which the republic of the universe created by God and in God is dispersed through many different mansions, that is, according to degrees of merits and graces. That house is Christ, who embraces all things with his power, disposes providence, rules with justice, orders with grace, contains for eternity, fills with wisdom, perfects with deification, "for from him and through him and in him and with him are all things" (Rom 11:36).[65]

Therefore, the degrees of the final participation emerge from the manner in which one shares in Christ. In the end, "the glory of the just will not be in the clarity of the body, but in the purity of contemplation, by which God will be seen face to face; nor will the misery of the impious be in the filthiness of his members, but in the privation of divine vision."[66] What counts is the manner of one's relationship with Christ.

Eriugena highlights the importance of taking on the *forma Verbi* in regard to one's final state: "For each one, according to the height of his sanctity and wisdom, will be formed by the one and the same form that all things seek, that is, the Word. . . . This form, since it is one and the same and remains incommunicable, will nevertheless be seen in multiple ways by those who are allowed to dwell in it. For each one, as we said, will

---

freedom, and possibility of returning to him, in whose image we are made, are given to the interior virtue of each one of us." *Expo.* X, iv, 151, 614–21.

65. *Peri.* V, 173–74, 5636–52.

66. *Peri.* V, 179, 5830–33.

possess knowledge of the only-begotten Word in himself, to the degree that grace will be given to him."[67] In the end, the goal of the spiritual ascent is the impression of the Word, the formation through the contemplation of Christ: "For every spirit, whether rational or intellectual, is unformed in itself; but if it should convert toward its cause, that is, toward the Word through which all things are made, then it is formed. There is, therefore, only one form of all rational and intellectual spirits: the Word of God. But if a spirit is irrational, it is similarly unformed in itself and then formed by the fantasies of sensible things."[68]

Fallen man, therefore, must take on the *forma Verbi* through ascetical practice and the reception of grace: man seeks to know the Word and to take on his likeness. This means embracing the pattern established within the great theophany, the Incarnation of the Son of God. Jesus reveals in himself the manner in which one turns from the corrupted world in its false autonomy toward authentic being in the unity of God. Thus Eriugena declares: "The perfect man is Christ, in whom all things are consummated. The fulfillment of his age is the consummation of the salvation of the universal Church, which is built among angels and men."[69] The final chapter examines the formation of this "perfect man" through the participation in the life of Christ.

---

67. *Peri.* I, 12, 270–78.
68. *Peri.* I, 47, 1384–90.
69. *Peri.* IV, 4, 39–42.

5

The Mystical Appropriation
of the Life of Jesus

CONTEMPORARY SCHOLARS CRITICIZE ERIUGENA'S FAILURE to take into account the historical Jesus. The incarnate Word, they say, is not a personality
with whom the believer can relate, but a vague intellectual concept, or a
mere spark to jump-start the return of all things to God. In the end, one
might even call his Christology "docetic," since the Word hardly exhibits
an authentic humanity. Overall, the lacuna of the historical Jesus is just
one symptom of Eriugena's "conspicuous depreciations of the reality of
the physical world, his departure from the idea of a divine economy that
operates in time, his elimination of the principle of synergy and his lack of
interest in the ecclesiastical and sacramental dimensions of Christ's saving
action."[1]

One may, of course, lament the fact that Eriugena is not Maximus the
Confessor. Yet rather than assume that Eriugena failed to incorporate the
central tenets of his Greek mentors, it would be better to examine his work
more widely in order to see just how he understood the importance of the
historicity of the Incarnation in the divine economy. History does, in fact,
have meaning for the Irishman, since it is the essential gateway to eternity: the Word-made-flesh acts within history in order to draw all things
to God.[2]

1. Colish, "Christology," 149.
2. "His [Eriugena's] faith imposed on him the belief in a God who reveals Himself

This chapter demonstrates that Eriugena's presentation of Jesus's life aims to inspire the mystical participation of believers in their own temporal journey. Eriugena highlights man's spiritual growth and participation in the divine: one must share in God through action and knowledge, struggle and contemplation. Now we shall see how one assumes Jesus's pattern of ascent.

The Historical Jesus

As it has already been shown, Eriugena's Christology is hardly docetic: the Word truly became one with man in his fallen state. This also means that the Word, by becoming flesh, entered history, time, and space, for time and space emerge with things that are created.[3] Jesus did not come as a phantom, a mere conceptual theophany, but as an actor in the drama of redemption.[4]

The historical events of Jesus's life genuinely reveal God and the manner in which human beings relate to God. John the Evangelist first saw the glory of the Word incarnate not through an interior vision, but through "the eyes of the body" in particular temporal encounters.[5] Christ, "the light that has come into the world," forms and judges the world through the historical events of his life:

> If the light had not come into the world, there would be no judgment of the world, as the Lord says: "If I had not come and spoken, they would not have sinned" (John 15:22). Thus the light—that is the *Incarnation of the Word of God, his teaching, his passion, and his resurrection*—judges the world. Whoever wants to approach the light, that is, the Son of God, in order that he might believe in Him and know Him, is not judged. Whoever, however, does not believe in Him and understand Him, will remain in the darkness

---

in history. The return of mankind to his divine origin—allegorically expressed in the parables of the Lost Sheep or in that of the Prodigal Son—takes place in history, a history called precisely the history of salvation." Jeauneau, "Neoplatonic Themes," 20.

3. See *Peri.* I, 39, 1131–32; 1135–36; *Hom.* VII, 236, 3–5.

4. Thus Eriugena speaks of the need for faith in the historical deeds (*fides rerum gestarum*) recounted in the Scriptures. See *Comm.* VI, ii, 332, 30–31; VI, v, 352, 33–35.

5. John first truly saw Jesus's glory on Mount Tabor: "Where did you see, oh blessed theologian, the glory of the incarnate Word? When did you see him? With what eyes did you perceive him? With corporeal eyes, I believe, on the mountain, at the time of the Transfiguration." *Hom.* XII, 308, 2–5.

and he will be damned in it, that is, he will be judged for not wanting to approach the light.[6]

Jesus's *entire* life—"his teachings, his passion, his resurrection"—forms the believer. Beginning with the historical Christ, one chooses to approach the light of the Incarnation or to reject it. The judgment of the world requires the Word's entry into history.

The Value of History in Relation to Spirit

Eriugena's approach to the relationship between history and spirit is best illustrated through his understanding of the Scriptures and the sacraments. In regard to the Scriptures, he makes the traditional distinction between "letter" and "spirit." The literal sense—the letter—of the Scriptures, expressing that which the carnal senses may grasp, conveys a genuine meaning: historical deeds (*res gestae*) and words. Yet Eriugena recognizes that such deeds and words lack stability and are, to some extent, temporally bound. Though *real* and necessary, they exist primarily as a gateway to the essential reality of the spiritual: "Indeed, the first step in the ascent to the height of virtue is the letter of Sacred Scriptures and the species of invisible things, in order that, having begun with the reading of the letter and the contemplation of creation, they might then ascend by steps of right reason to the spirit of the letter and the rational principles of creation."[7] Words and deeds, therefore, are real symbols that allow man to make the *transitus* to the essential divine truths.[8]

Eriugena's reading of the Israelites' flight from Egypt illustrates the relationship between history and spirit. In this passage, he highlights the essential spiritual state of the reader for perceiving the deeper reality behind the events narrated in the Scriptures:

> For example, one may read the book of *Genesis* [*sic*], in that place where it relates the carnal crossing (*transitus*) of Israel through the Red Sea. The simple Christian, still reclining, so to speak, on the field of temporal and carnal things, is nourished by history alone, since whatever is done there is grasped by the corporeal senses: for

6. *Comm.* III, vi, 234–36, 51–60.

7. *Comm.* VI, iii, 338, 11–15.

8. One also finds this *transitus* through the Scriptures in Maximus the Confessor's idea of διάβασις. See Maximus, *Ambigua* X, 112B–113B. Also see Blowers, *Exegesis*, 112–17.

the Israelites are *seen* crossing the sea with dry feet; the Egyptians truly are killed. This was also *heard* by nearby peoples; the wave of the sea is *tasted, smelled and touched.* The soul that is still simple and faithful takes all these things with him and ponders them, as one who is satisfied by some fragments of divine history. Since the simple cannot grasp the understanding of the letter itself, those who are able to know spiritual things gather the understanding [of the letter] in order that it may not perish and may profit those capable of understanding.[9]

History consists of genuine events that engage the five senses and form the faithful hearers. On the one hand, the simple faithful who read the Scriptures at the historical level through faith do not nourish themselves with phantoms—the events are true; nor are the simple faithful debased individuals because they only ponder history through the lens of faith. These believers, rather, seek to grow by pondering the mighty deeds of God in the heart and searching for the deeper meaning behind them. God works in history and in the narrative of history in order that the faithful may discover the inner depths of the divine plan.

On the other hand, even "those who are able to know spiritual things," that is, those who enter into the spiritual meaning of the Scriptures, still depend upon the historical deeds and words: they gather the spiritual meaning from the "fragments" of history. Yet their maturity in the Christian way of life allows them to perceive the deeper meaning behind the scriptural narrative. They are capable of seeing truths that lead one from the carnal to the essential.[10]

This interaction between history and spirit applies to the sacraments as well. The sacraments, through signs and symbols perceptible to the senses of the faithful, lead one to the hidden realities of God. When, for example, Eriugena speaks of the body and blood of the Lord in the New Testament, he notes that "the mystery is accomplished on the level of historical deeds,

9. *Comm.* VI, vi, 360, 39–52. This passage is found within a longer discussion of Jesus's feeding of the five-thousand.

10. Eriugena notes that some passages in the Scriptures, such as Jesus's discourses in John, do not admit a "historical" reading, but only an allegorical or spiritual: the distinction between *allegoria dicti et facti* and *allegoria dicti sed non facti*. Such passages that do not relate historical deeds are symbols, perceived only by seeing or hearing. "Thus in the symbols, that is, in the dictations of spiritual doctrine, which is handed on by the allegory of discourse and not of deed, no fragments are collected, since it is not divided into history and understanding. For the understanding alone is grasped in it, not the deed." *Comm.* VI, vi, 364, 76–81. Also see McGinn, "Originality," 66–67.

while the spiritual understanding is discovered according to the hidden sense."[11] Those who still see "according to the flesh" experience the Eucharist through the gift of faith; the mature grasp the hidden meaning through the spiritual intelligence: "The spiritual fragment is for those who are able to know the height of the divine understandings of the mystery itself, and, therefore, they gather it in order that it may not perish. For the mystery formed from letter and spirit in part perishes and in part remains eternally. That which perishes is seen, because it is sensible and temporal; that which remains is not seen, because it is spiritual and eternal."[12]

Far from disparaging man's temporal and material existence, Eriugena teaches that history is, in fact, a theophany of God. Though that which man perceives through the senses, because it is unstable and ephemeral, can never adequately convey the truth of things, nonetheless it offers a genuine gateway to contemplation.[13] One cannot ignore, therefore, the life of Jesus. The history of the Word-made-flesh shapes man's action and contemplation during the journey of the return to God.

The Life of Christ

This section examines Eriugena's treatment of key events in Jesus's life. He never questions the historicity of these moments and, particularly in the poetry, describes them with great reverence. His movement toward the deeper, spiritual significance begins with the reality of the event itself. Most of all, however, he wants the reader to assume the mystery behind the historical event. As Bernard McGinn has noted, "Eriugena has his own version of the traditional *imitatio Christi* theme, though for him this is not the literal imitation found in many later Western mystics, but is rather a following of Christ's example in lifting up our minds in contemplation to enjoy spiritual food."[14] Eriugena desires that one participate in the historical life of Jesus in order to share in mystical experience, in the transformative relationship with God.

---

11. *Comm.* VI, vi, 364, 82–85. I am adopting Jeauneau's translation of *cerebrum*. On the manuscript problem and the meaning of this word see *Comm.*, 364, n. 9.

12. *Comm.* VI, vi, 366, 90–96. On the Eucharist as mystery see Pépin, "Mysteria," 17–18.

13. On the falsity of transient speech see Marler, "Scriptural Truth," 162–63.

14. McGinn, "Mysticus," 252.

The Birth of Jesus

"The Word became flesh and was born of the Virgin Mary."[15] In affirming this teaching, Eriugena points toward the reality of the Incarnation. The salvation and restoration of man begins with the birth of the Word:

> Thus, born into the world, he suffered under the law of evil men.
> He himself destroyed my death by his own death.[16]

One starts with this historical reality of Christ's birth and ascends to its deeper truths. The Evangelist John, for instance, begins his Gospel by saying that "the Word-God was made man from the Virgin, while still being in all things in a supernatural way."[17] Next, however, John ascends and proclaims that "the same Word was superessentially born of the Father before and beyond all things."[18] The historical Virgin birth, therefore, points toward the truth of the eternal birth of the Word in the Trinity.

Eriugena, in his reading of the *Celestial Hierarchy,* reflects upon the birth of Jesus and the wondrous missions of the angels. God informs the angels of Jesus's birth in advance in order that they may proclaim the mystery to humanity.[19] Gabriel could then tell Mary of how, "within her, the divine mystery of the ineffable formation of the Word of God would take place."[20] Another angel appeared to prepare Joseph for his mission, and a multitude of heavenly hosts "shared with the inhabitants of the earth that truly praiseworthy *doxologia,* that is, a song of praise: 'Glory to God in the highest and on earth peace to men of good will' (Luke 2:14)."[21]

Eriugena, drawing upon the thought of Gregory of Nazianzus and Maximus the Confessor,[22] describes the "four births" of humanity that Christ assumes and perfects.[23] The first birth of man is primordial: "All of

15. *Expo.* II, v, 49, 1068–71.

16. *Carm.* V, 76, 19–20.

17. John 1:14a: "And the Word became flesh and dwelt among us, full of grace and truth."

18. John 1:14b: "We have beheld his glory, glory as of the only-begotten Son from the Father." *Hom.* V, 224–26, 23–27.

19. *Expo.* IV, iii, 79, 561–74.

20. *Expo.* IV, iii, 80, 597–99.

21. *Expo.* IV, iii, 80, 619–22.

22. See Gregorius Nazianzenus, *Orationes* XL, 2, 198–200, 14–17; Maximus, *Ambigua* XLII, 1316A–B.

23. *Comm.* III, i, 204, 65–68.

human kind was born at once from nothing."[24] By humiliating himself and becoming man, the Word recapitulates the original *creatio ex nihilo* of man and becomes the authentic theophany of God. Jesus is perfect humanity and the restoration of divine glory.

The second birth "followed from man's crime and comes from the two sexes, in the manner of the animals, concerning which the same Scripture says, 'He made them masculine and feminine' (Gen 5:2). Through this all human kind is multiplied infinitely according to earthly succession."[25] Man suffers this kind of painful birth because of his sinfulness and rejection of God. Yet the Word freely chooses to take on this fallen existence in Bethlehem, when he is born of Mary and accepts the temporal limitations of fallen humanity. In this birth, one sees the true solidarity of the divine Son with the brokenness of creation.

The third birth comes from the Spirit, "in which human nature begins to return by birth to the original seat from which it fled."[26] This rebirth requires the sacrament of baptism and a turning from the deceptions of the world toward spiritual truths. Jesus demonstrates this truth by submitting to the baptism of John and rendering the sacrament potent through his own death and resurrection. He is the first born of the Spirit.

Finally, the fourth birth "will be in the resurrection of all things, when our entire nature is born at once into eternal life, when death is destroyed."[27] Jesus assumes this birth through is own death and resurrection, conquering the power of sin in the world. He restores the potential of man's nature and offers the efficacious grace for the resurrection of all humanity.[28]

The participatory nature of this analysis becomes evident in Eriugena's summary statement regarding the four births that Jesus assumes: "The first birth is natural, the second exists because of sin, the third comes through the grace of the redeemer, the fourth is according to nature and grace. For the power of the resurrection is present naturally to human nature, since eternal death is contrary to it."[29] Jesus's assumption of man's four "births" renders them effective and transformative: the four births are now modes of participation in Jesus's life and gateways to salvation. Just as the Word-

24. *Comm.* III, i, 204, 68–71.

25. *Comm.* III, i, 204, 71–75.

26. *Comm.* III, i, 204, 75–79.

27. *Comm.* III, i, 204, 79–81.

28. *Comm.* III, i, 206, 83–85.

29. *Comm.*, III, i, 204–6, 81–85.

made-flesh passed through these births, so must each and every person follows the same path. The Incarnation empowers man once again to become a full sharer in the divine and to be born again "according to nature and grace."

John the Baptist and the Baptism of Jesus

John the Baptist, according to Eriugena, was the forerunner because his entire life foreshadowed important moments of Jesus's own life: John's miraculous birth to elderly parents pointed toward the miracle of the virgin birth; his powerful preaching in the desert readied the people for Jesus's transformative words; his baptisms in the Jordan with water pointed toward the baptism by fire and the Spirit in Christ.[30] John was the forerunner also because he was the prophet charged with the mission to announce the coming of Jesus and he knew of Christ's coming in advance. Eriugena has John declare: "Before I saw him, who was born in the flesh in the order of time after my own birth, I saw him while I was still in the womb of my sterile mother in a prophetic vision: I saw him before me, made man in the womb of the virgin."[31] John, as a prophet, knew Jesus's identity and the scope of his mission in advance in order to form the people for the reception of the Son of God.

Through this vision, John accepted his vocation to preach faith in Christ and the hope in the resurrection. He proclaimed the belief in Christ by declaring "make straight the way of the Lord," since "the way" refers to faith in Jesus: "For there is no other way the Lord enters human hearts except through faith, which is the way of the Lord."[32] Eriugena also asserts that John's preaching anticipated the resurrection from the dead, since the Pharisees, who supported this teaching, came to hear John.[33] John, therefore, sought to direct others toward Jesus and to preach hope in the resurrection.

---

30. In effect, Jesus recapitulates and perfects all aspects of John's mission. "Indeed the forerunner was obliged to fulfill his mission as forerunner in all things in order that, just as he preceded Christ by birth and preaching, so also by the similarity of his baptism." *Comm.* III, viii, 244, 19–22.

31. *Hom.* XVI, 278, 7–10. Also see *Hom.* XVI, 278, 2–10.

32. *Comm.* I, xxviii, 144, 5–9.

33. *Comm.* I, xxviii, 146, 34–44.

John also revealed the manner of deification through grace and action. John's very name means "he who is graced,"[34] that is, one who has been called to be elevated to the divine. The pattern of his life—ascetic living, preaching, and martyrdom—manifested the true light of the Word and the potential of man:

> Thus the forerunner of the Lord was a man, not God; the Lord, however, of whom he was the forerunner, was at the same time both man and God. The forerunner was a man who would pass into (*transiturus*) God by grace; the one whom he preceded was God by nature and would assume man through humility and the desire for our salvation and redemption. . . . "To him was given the name of John" (Luke 1:63), that is, to him was given [the grace] of becoming the precursor of the King of Kings, the revealer of the Word incarnate and the baptizer into spiritual son-ship. He was a witness for the eternal light by his voice and by his martyrdom.[35]

John, by his way of life, shows the path of one called to "pass into God," that is, to be deified. His baptism adumbrates the divine adoption offered to humanity in Christ.

Eriugena confronts the difficult question regarding the significance and effectiveness of John's baptism. He makes it clear that the baptism of John in no way realized the remission of original or personal sin: for this the people would have to await the baptism of Christ.[36] Yet Eriugena maintains that John's baptism had great meaning and offers a response that Thomas Aquinas would later cite in his *Summa*: "For just as the teachings of the faith are profitable for the catechumens who have not yet been baptized, so the baptism of John is profitable for those baptized by him before they underwent the baptism of Christ."[37] John's baptism, therefore, formed the people for the reception of the Word incarnate: "For as the dawn precedes the rising of the sun, so the sacraments of John precede the works of Christ; and, as the dawn dispels in a certain way the shadows, so the teaching and mystery of the forerunner began to disperse the darkness and ignorance of the whole world."[38]

34. See *Hom.* II, 208, 1–3.

35. *Hom.* XV, 276, 17–22; 26–28.

36. *Comm.* III, viii, 242–44, 4–6.

37. *Comm.* III, viii, 244, 7–10. Also see Thomas Aquinas, *ST* III, q. 38, art. 1.

38. *Comm.* III, viii, 244, 22–26.

Why, however, did Jesus undergo the baptism of John—a baptism that the people experienced as a sign of repentance? Eriugena explores a number of reasons. First, Jesus did this to honor John and to testify to the world that John's call to repentance was authentic. In effect, Jesus verified John's catechesis by submitting to the immersion in the Jordan: "The humility of the Lord was sufficient to give praise and witness to the servant's baptism."[39]

Second, Jesus underwent baptism in order effect "a certain sanctification of the baptism of John." Thus John's own baptism becomes effective only through the immersion of Christ.[40] This interpretation follows an ancient theme, in which Christ blesses the waters of the world through his immersion into the Jordan.[41]

The third, and perhaps the most striking, reason that Eriugena offers comes from unspecified Greek sources:

> Yet we know that Greek authors faithfully assert that the sanctification of the humanity of Christ was increased through the sacrament of the baptism of John. They argue this primarily by pointing toward the descent of the Holy Spirit in the form of a dove upon the one who was baptized. This is not surprising, since the Evangelist said: "But Jesus was growing in wisdom and age and grace before God and men" (Luke 2:52). What is remarkable if Christ received a certain increase of his humanity through the sacrament of baptism by his forerunner because of, for example, his humility, by which he did not refuse to submit to the baptism by his servant? He received grace in order that, by virtue of his baptism, all those who believe in him might assume the remission of all crimes, both original and personal.[42]

Eriugena's adoption of this reading is significant. The "increase in the humanity of Christ" occurred not only through divine action—the reception of grace—but also by Jesus's free human submission to ritual immersion. The augmentation of Jesus's human nature occurred "because of

---

39. *Comm.* III, viii, 246, 32–35.

40. *Comm.* III, viii, 246, 46–48.

41. See, for instance, Ephraem the Syrian: "Blessed are you, little Jordan River, into which the Flowing Sea descended and was baptized. . . . Blessed are your torrents, cleansed by His descent. For the Holy One, Who condescended to bathe in you, descended to open by His baptism the baptism for the pardoning of souls." Ephraem the Syrian, *Hymns on Virginity,* in Ferguson, *Baptism,* 503. On this theme see Jensen, *Baptismal,* 11; Blowers, *Drama,* 251–57.

42. *Comm.* III, viii, 246–48, 49–62.

his humility," the self-emptying manifested in his assumption of the sin of humanity: he became more fully "human"—his humanity more truly "is"—in his humble relationship with the Father, in contrast to recalcitrant and broken humanity in its fallen state. This then rendered him open to the reception of grace on behalf of humanity, drawing all persons into his expiation of original and personal sins. In this interpretation of the baptism, Jesus acted as God and man, growing more authentically human on man's behalf.

Finally, Eriugena cites a justification by Augustine. Augustine notes that the baptized, recognizing the great gift that they have received, may become complacent or even proud in living their faith. Jesus's baptism took place as an example for them: "But in order that they not wander into this error and work in vain, the Lord wanted to give an example to them through his own baptism, so that none of them would dare to be puffed up when they saw their own Lord submit to the baptism of his servant."[43] Jesus's baptism anticipated the needs and weaknesses of the future faithful by giving them an example of humility.

Eriugena's reading of this significant and mysterious moment in the life of Christ aims to inspire an appropriation on the part of believers. He not only wants to address the exegetical problem of the Christ's submission to baptism for the remission of sins, but also to show how to bridge the gap between the historical event and the life of the believer. The Christian who receives the grace of baptism grows in the authentic humanity of Jesus through humility, as the paired readings from the unknown Greek authors and Augustine show. Jesus teaches through example in order that humanity may find fulfillment through abandonment to God and the reception of transformative grace.

The Public Life of Jesus

Eriugena does not ignore the active years of Jesus's life. The Incarnation does not deify man through a unification of two natures as if it were a simple chemical reaction, but rather his entire life reforms creation. In fact, the Word-made-flesh has a mission to fulfill that comprises a variety of salvific activities.

---

43. *Comm.* III, viii, 248, 66–70. Also see Augustinus, *In Johannis Evangelium* XIII, 6, 133–34, 10–24.

Preaching

Jesus came to preach the word of God. Jesus stands out as more than a prophet, since he is the subject of his own proclamation:

> "The one whom God sent, he speaks the words of God" (John 3:34). This seems to say: "The one whom God sent, he speaks the words of the God who sends him." The prophets, as well as the apostles, did this. What great thing, therefore, is given to Christ, that was not given to others? Hear the words: "The one who was sent by God"—that is, God the Father—"speaks the words of God." Since that one who was sent is God, he speaks the words of God, meaning: The one whom God sent is perfectly God and for this reason his words are of God. Therefore, the words that belong to the Son of God, through which he testifies that he is God, are the words of God. The words of the prophets and the apostles are the words of God, because they spoke the words of God—for the Holy Spirit spoke in them. Those words did not refer back to the speakers, so that they might be their own words, but they are the words of the true God.[44]

The prophets and apostles point towards Jesus; Jesus directs the faithful towards himself. The Son, as head of the church, manifests the entirety of God's Spirit and shares the plenitude of God's gifts through his preaching and personal witness.[45]

Eriugena frequently examines Jesus's preaching, especially his parables, in order to give ways for appropriating Christ's life. The parable of the Prodigal Son, for example, is an allegory for humanity's fall and return. Though man abandoned God to squander the goods of his nature on selfish living, the Father embraces him when he repents and comes back. The price for this reconciliation, however, is the incarnate Word:

> But afterwards the son [man] will return to the Father and will receive the first (*primam*) stole, that is, the pristine (*primum*) garment of nature. In addition, he will receive the garment of virtue (symbolized by the ring), as well as the reward from the death of Christ (which is symbolized by the sandals on his feet), that is, eternal life, which is restored universally to humanity by the death of the Lord. And the fattened calf is brought in and killed. And

---

44. *Comm.* III, xii, 270–72, 5–19. Also see Augustinus, *In Johannis Evangelium* XIV, x–xi, 148, 1–31; 149, 1–16.

45. *Comm.* III, xii, 272, 19–21. Also see *Expo.* II, v, 47, 108–1012.

who is this calf, if not the man, Christ, full of the seven-fold grace of the Holy Spirit, and certainly made thick through the fat of the letter and visible nature?[46]

Repentant humanity's approach to the Father, therefore, depends upon both conversion and the salvific actions of the Word-made-flesh. The transformation of the Son unfolds step-by-step, moving from repentance to virtue, from virtue to the new life in the risen Jesus.

Another example, the parable of the Good Shepherd, lends itself naturally to a christological interpretation. In Eriugena's reading, the incarnate Word restores the perfection of broken humanity.

> In a similar way, understand the story of the hundredth sheep, which abandoned the celestial flock and wandered. The Good Shepherd, who is Christ, sought him and found him. Taking him upon his shoulders, he brought him back to the flock, which he, the lost sheep, had abandoned by wandering. This is numbered the hundredth for a special reason, since, after the Fall of human nature, the perfection (which is understood by the number one hundred) of the heavenly Jerusalem, "which is our mother" (Gal 4:26), is diminished. Its number, as one hundred, will be fulfilled when human kind will return to it in its head, which is Christ.[47]

God's desire for unity truly is all-inclusive: perfection requires the entirety of the flock. Jesus, the good shepherd, yearns to bring all into himself.

In a final example, the explication of the parable of the Wise and Foolish Virgins, Eriugena discovers the diversity of manners in which man approaches Christ. The ten virgins, who represent the totality of humanity as moved by a natural and intelligible affection, seek "the one who loves them." Yet, "although the motion of rational nature toward its end, that is, Christ, is common to all, and the appetite for the eternal light, which is symbolized by the lamps, is shared by all, nevertheless [humanity] does not equally share in that light 'which illuminates every man coming into this world' (John 1:9)."[48] Like the wise and foolish virgins, each person approaches Christ differently, depending upon his natural gifts and the graces received. Eriugena sees three final modes of participation after humanity's reunion with God: 1) some will be deified because of their virtues and openness to grace; 2) others, who lack perfection, will rejoice only in natural goods;

46. *Peri.* V, 203, 6569–81.
47. *Peri.* V, 204–5, 6610–19.
48. *Peri.* V, 212, 6876–80.

3) and still others will suffer through their eternal adherence to deceptive phantasies.[49] The final participation in Christ, therefore, will vary, depending upon the state of the believer.[50]

Eriugena's interpretation of these parables illustrates important elements of mystical participation in Christ. On the one hand, one must follow Jesus through a concrete conversion of life: one's mode of participation depends upon moral rectitude. On the other hand, the believer must receive the saving actions of Jesus—the good shepherd—in order to be healed and raised up.

The Miracles and Wondrous Deeds of Jesus

Jesus also formed the faithful through his miracles and wondrous deeds. "For we, whom He chose from the world, see his glory in his most evident miracles, in the Transfiguration on the spiritual mountain, the clarity of the resurrection; there is no other glory, but the glory of the first born of the Father."[51] The mighty deeds of the Lord reveal the truth and shape the vision of the faithful.

THE FEEDING OF THE 5,000 (JOHN 6:1–14)

Eriugena's exegesis of the feeding of the five thousand in the Gospel of John draws especially from the treatments of Augustine, Maximus, and perhaps even Origen.[52] Yet he develops his interpretation around the main theme of the movement from letter to spirit, or from action to contemplation. In fact, Jesus, in this Gospel scene, teaches by his words and deeds that one must turn the self from the carnal toward spiritual realities.

Jesus initiates this reorientation when he looks upward: "Lifting up his eyes, then, and seeing that a multitude was coming to him, Jesus said to

---

49. See *Peri.* V, 212, 6884–95.

50. Eriugena gives a similar interpretation to the parable of the Rich Man and Lazarus (Luke 16:19–31): the divide between Lazarus in Abraham's bosom and the sufferings of the rich man is not physical, but rather moral. The two differ by their manners of participation. See *Peri.* V, 172–73, 5609–20.

51. *Comm.* I, xxii, 102, 1–5.

52. See Origenes, *In Genesim* VII, v–vi, 206–10; Augustinus, *In Johannis Evangelium* XXIV, 244–48; Maximus, *Ambigua* LXVI, 1369B–1404C.

Philip, 'How are we to buy bread, so that these people may eat' (John 6:5)?"
His movement indicates the significance of the miracle to come:

> Then he raises his eyes, teaching us to raise the eyes of our heart
> and teaching the whole world to run together from all direc-
> tions toward faith in Christ. Thus we are advised by the example
> of Christ to raise the eyes of our heart in order that, if, after he
> teaches us and illuminates us interiorly, we should be allowed to
> ascend to the height of action, knowledge and theology, then the
> crowd of subsequent carnal thoughts may not disturb us and hurl
> us from the height of contemplation. We then may take care to
> pasture our thoughts in a satisfying way—to the extent that it is
> possible—with spiritual food.[53]

In this simple gesture Jesus summarizes the path that the faithful must
follow: 1) action, that is, growth in virtue, or *praktike*; 2) knowledge, that is,
movement from sensible symbols to spiritual truths, or *physike*; and 3) theology or perfect contemplation, that is, experience of and union with God,
or *theologia*. In fact, the literal sense (*iuxta fidem rerum gestarum*)[54] of the
miraculous multiplication illuminates this path from action to theology,
from deeds to contemplation. One cannot remain at the level of action and
knowledge, but must always seek the higher grace of mystical contemplation: "Indeed the action of the virtues only purges the souls of the faithful
and knowledge of created things illuminates them. Yet the purgation and
illumination are not enough for them, unless the habit of perfect contemplation is added, which alone leads souls to the full plenitude of spiritual
refreshment."[55] Jesus conveys the essential path to divine union: asceticism,
contemplation of nature and the Scriptures, and the gifted contemplation
of God.

This ascent from action to theology also requires the church founded
by Jesus. Eriugena makes this evident through his interpretation of the
distribution of the five loaves to the crowd. In effect, Jesus establishes
the structure and mission of the church through his instructions to the
disciples: the ministers of the church distribute the sacraments (concrete,
historically rooted signs that convey spiritual truths) and symbols (Christ's
words that draw one into higher contemplation) to the hungry faithful:

53. *Comm.* VI, i, 326–28, 7–16.
54. *Comm.* VI, ii, 332, 30–31.
55. *Comm.* VI, ii, 330, 19–25.

> The five loaves and two fishes are brought to this multitude hungering for the faith of Christ, that is, the *sacraments*, which are the deeds and written discourses [of Scripture], and the *symbols*, which are only the things said, and not the deeds. Christ receives the five loaves and two fishes and, giving thanks to the Father, who wants to nourish his faithful with symbols and sacraments, hands them over to his disciples, that is, his teachers and ministers. They divide the fragments among the crowd. They break up the barley loaves, that is, they divide the mysteries of each Law [of the Old and New Testament] into deeds (*res gestas*) and their spiritual meanings (*spirituales intellectus*).[56]

Jesus, therefore, establishes a means of transmission for his words and deeds in history through the preaching and teaching of his faithful ministers.[57] The miracle and its circumstances represent Jesus's extension of himself in history—through sacraments and symbols—in order that the faithful might participate in him.

Eriugena never puts the historicity of the miracle into question, nor does he ignore the details in favor of a complete "spiritualization." Rather, the miracle teaches a program of life for every believer that incorporates asceticism, prayer, and the mission of the church. Christ nourishes the believer by guiding him to a mystical participation in his life.

THE TRANSFIGURATION (MATT 17:1–8)

The transfiguration stands out as a prime example of Jesus's wondrous acts. The disciples' vision of Jesus's glory, in which the Lord appears with Elijah and Moses, manifests three states of human existence: 1) the present life of the flesh, that is, Elijah, who did not die but was taken into heaven; 2) the intermediate state of souls before the general resurrection, that is, Moses, who did die and now lives in the intermediate state; and 3) the resurrected state itself, that is, Jesus as he appears in his glory.[58] On Mount Tabor the disciples witness a revelation not according to the laws of nature, but

---

56. *Comm.* VI, vi, 358, 25–34.

57. On the distinctions between the reception by the "carnal" and the "spiritual" see *Comm.* VI, vi, 358–60, 34–39.

58. "The most evident of these three modes are revealed in the Transformation of the Lord on the mountain: the type of those living in the flesh is Elijah, the type of those freed of the body is Moses, and the type of those rising from the dead is the Lord himself." *Peri.* V, 194–95, 6315–18.

according to the divine will to reveal the unity of these states in the person of Christ.[59]

The transfiguration, therefore, reveals that all the states of man's participation in the one risen Lord. Though the vision begins with three men, it concludes with only one:

> Do not think that Elijah, while still living in his body, came from some localized paradise; or that Moses, as if his body were restored, then came to Christ from some realm of the souls; or that they [Elijah and Moses], when the mystery of the Transfiguration was over, returned to those places whence they came. But believe and understand faithfully and without hesitation, that they came from no other place than from him with whom they appeared on the mountain, and in whom they were before they appeared, and whom they did not abandon when they appeared, and into whom, when the sacrament of the appearance was over, they returned—not in another direction, but into the very One in whom and with whom they are one. This is clearly shown through the three chosen disciples in the mystery of the Transfiguration, who, "when they raised their eyes, saw no one except Jesus alone" (Matt 17:8).[60]

The transfiguration, like all of the wondrous deeds and miracles in the life of Jesus, occurs to clear man's vision and to open him to the mystery of the one Christ. Here Eriugena desires that the reader understand him- or herself as a participant in Christ even now—as Elijah, who is in the flesh, participates in Christ—and that the unity continues after death (the intermediate state) and in the resurrected state. The transfiguration makes a theoretical teaching—the unity of all states of human participation in the Word—a perceptible truth for the believer.

---

59. The manner in which the soul of Moses became visible in the transfiguration goes beyond any natural laws. See *Peri.* III, 62, 1766–79.

60. *Peri.* V, 195, 6320–32. Ambrose's treatment of the transfiguration also stresses the importance of unity in Christ: "Thus although there were three, they were made one. Three are seen in the beginning, but one in the end; for by perfect faith they are one. And so the Lord asked the Father for this: that we might be one (John 17:21). Not only Moses and Elijah are one in Christ, but also we are the one body of Christ. Therefore, they also are received into the body of Christ, because we will be one in Christ Jesus. Or, perhaps, because the law and the prophets from the Word—which, however, began from the Word—conclude in the Word: 'The end of the law is Christ as justice for all who believe' (Rom 10:4)." Ambrosius, *In Lucam*, VII, xx, 222, 232–40.

Conflicts and the Formation of the Church

Jesus's public life was not without its moments of conflict and controversy. For instance, the Pharisees sought to eliminate Jesus because of the growing success of his ministry and his increasing number of disciples. Jesus does not place himself in danger before his time, but rather avoids the Pharisees until the moment designated by God. "He does this not because he is afraid or powerless . . . but to leave an example for those who would believe in Him, giving to them his example—the power of fleeing in the face of those persecuting them and leaving them for a time—lest before the hour pleasing to and chosen by God, they should be seized by the persecutors."[61] Jesus, even while facing his encroaching passion and death, focuses upon the needs of future believers and the dangers of persecution. Their martyrdom, like his own death, may only occur at the moment the Father designates for the sake of the gospel.

In all of his public actions Jesus effectively raises up the church, since he is the builder (*fabricator*) of the church, which consists of Jews and Gentiles.[62] Jesus initiates the formation of the church with the Jews, his own people, because "Christ, who is the salvation of the world, is from the Jews, not only by origin of the flesh, but also by being a progeny of their faith: the faith and the primitive Church arose from them."[63] Yet after establishing the church among the Jews,[64] Jesus extends the calling to the Gentiles, as shown by his request for water from the Samaritan woman at the well (John 4:7): "Jesus, sitting upon the well, seeks the drink of faith from the primitive Church, which he had chosen from the Gentiles: by this faith the primitive Church believes in him."[65] The incarnate Word receives the transforming Spirit for the sake of humanity: "In Christ, who is the head of the Church, God does not give his Spirit in a measure, but as a whole. For just as God [the Father] generated his Son from his whole self, so he gave to his incarnate Son his whole Spirit—not partially, not piecemeal, but generally and universally."[66]

---

61. *Comm.* IV, i, 278–80, 21–27.

62. *Comm.* IV, i, 282, 59–68.

63. *Comm.* IV, vii, 316, 36–41.

64. *Comm.* IV, i, 280, 27–34.

65. *Comm.* IV, iii, 294, 14–16. Eriugena states that the initial faith that Christ seeks comes from the Gentiles' capacity to reason. See *Comm.* IV, iii, 294, 16–18.

66. *Comm.* III, xii, 272, 30–34.

Eriugena, therefore, finds the foundation of the church in the life of Jesus. All must establish themselves in "that foundation, that is, God the Word, our Lord Jesus Christ, upon whom, like an unshakable rock, the universal Church of rational and intellectual creatures is being built."[67] The church calls all toward participation, in which Christ shares the transformative gift of the Spirit.

Christ's Passion, Death, and Descent into Hell

The previous chapter examined the passion and death of Jesus as one of the motives for the Incarnation: Christ came to die for the liberation of humanity from sin and death. Other moments in the history of Jesus's final hours led Eriugena to reflect upon the person of Jesus and the believer's participation in Jesus's sacrifice.

The Last Supper

In a reflection upon the Last Supper, Eriugena discusses the divisions that occur in humanity through free choice and merit. Judas and Peter represent the two responses to the incarnate Word:

> Indeed, one essence unites those whom differing merits divide. A little before the Lord was to suffer, Judas Iscariot and Simon Peter were dining with the Lord at the same time in the dining room: one was next to Christ, one was far from Christ. The one who dipped his hand with Christ into the dish was the betrayer of the humanity of Christ; the other, who was not said to have dipped his hand with Christ into the dish, was the contemplator of Christ's divinity. The greedy one sold the man-God; the other, a theologian, knew the God-man. One betrayed the body by the kiss of the body; the other loved the divine mind by a kiss of the mind. And so I say this: know that it is not the intervals of space, but the qualities of merits that make man approach Christ or move away from him.[68]

The Last Supper scene reveals the importance of contemplation for the follower of Jesus. Eriugena compares physical and spiritual distances from Christ, emphasizing that one truly approaches Christ through living

---

67. *Expo.* XV, v, 203, 572–75.
68. *Peri.* V, 173, 5623–36.

an authentic Christian life: contemplation and love bridge the physical-temporal chasm between the contemporary believer and the Lord. Like Peter, a Christian may draw near to Jesus by seeking the deeper contemplation of the Word.

In his *Expositiones in Ierarchiam Coelestem,* Eriugena discusses the sacrament of the Eucharist that Jesus established in the Last supper:

> Notice how he [pseudo-Dionysius] so beautifully and expressly asserts that this visible Eucharist, which the priests daily confect upon the altar from the sensible material of bread and wine, and which they receive corporeally after it has been confected and sanctified, is the likeness in type of the spiritual participation in Jesus, whom we taste by faith through the intellect alone, that is to say, we understand (*intelleximus*). We take it up into the interior bowels of our nature for the sake of our salvation, spiritual growth, and ineffable deification. It is right, therefore, he says, that the human mind, which is ascending from sensible things to the likeness and equality of the celestial powers, observe the most divine, visible Eucharist formed in the Church, which is the greatest type of participation in him. By the Eucharist, we now participate in Jesus through faith, and in the future we will participate by sight, and we will be united to him by charity.[69]

The Eucharist is the church's mode of participation in Jesus. In his comments, Eriugena emphasizes the physical reality of the sacrament: it must be seen and consumed in conjunction with the celebration of the rite. Yet the spiritual truth takes priority, since the sacrament transforms the believer from within. It penetrates the depths of broken human nature and allows one an anticipatory sharing in the future beatific vision and deifying union. The Eucharist established by Jesus gives man the gift of the divine life through a material-spiritual means that is appropriate to the limitations of the flesh.

The Passion of Jesus

Eriugena examines the problem of Christ's suffering in his two natures. He is careful not to attribute pain and death directly to Christ's divinity, while still recognizing the reality of Jesus's passion in the unity of substance or person:

69. *Expo.* I, iii, 16–17, 570–84.

Jesus, while hanging on the wood of the cross, commended the Spirit to the Father, saying: "Father, into your hands I commend my Spirit" (Luke 23:46). It is as if he had said: "I commend into your hands the Spirit proceeding from me and you, since it is impassible, while I alone suffer with the flesh. I alone received the flesh and was made flesh." Not because he himself is passible according to his divinity, but because the passibility, passion, and death of his humanity, which he alone received, is referred to him. He cosuffered (*compassus*) with the humanity that he had assumed to himself in the unity of substance [person]. Thus because he cosuffered [with the flesh], it is not incorrect to say, and to say truly, that he suffered; for the one substance [person] of the Word and man was not divided in the passion.[70]

Eriugena highlights the real agony of the divine-human subject, Jesus Christ. Though the divine nature of the Son remains "impassible," it still "co-suffers" (*compatior*) with his human nature. Eriugena denies that the divinity of Christ absents itself from the cross, while his humanity shares in the tortures like a suit that protects the Word from contamination. The hypostatic union—the union of substance or person—guarantees that the "co-suffering" is a genuine suffering in a divine-human manner: the one who suffers and dies is not a particular nature, but a person (*substantia*)—Jesus, the God-man.[71] Eriugena has learned the lessons of Chalcedon well, focusing upon the person, the distinct individual, not upon the natures, as the subject of Christ's passion and death.[72]

Eriugena describes the scene of the passion in the striking words of his poetry. The piercing of Christ's palms, the flowing blood and water, the crown of thorns—all of these images come to vivid life in his verses. He invites the reader to envision Jesus's final hour affixed to the wood:

---

70. *Peri.* IV, 6, 107–18.

71. Eriugena offers a lengthy citation from Epiphanius regarding the impassibility of Christ's divinity in the passion. Epiphanius, in fact, uses the image of a man putting on a bloody garment in order to explain the manner in which the divinity suffers in the humanity of Christ: Christ's humanity is a "suit" that protects the impassibility of the divinity. Yet Eriugena's emphasis on the "co-suffering" of the Word with the humanity, along with his stress upon the unity of substance or person, implies a more intimate union of the divine and human natures in the passion. God mysteriously and truly shares in the trial of the cross. "The divinity of the word is impassible and co-suffers with his humanity." *Peri.* IV, 9, 186–87. Also see Epiphanius, *Ancoratus*, 69, 144C–145A.

72. Regarding, however, the ambivalent outcome of Chalcedon in preserving the unity of Christ see Beeley, *Unity*, 307–9.

> Put before yourself the two thieves hanging from two trees:
> They were equal in their crime, they will be unequal by grace.
> One saw the borders of paradise with Christ,
> the other was plunged into the sulphurous Styx.
> The eclipse of the sun, the moon rising in the morning:
> there was a shadow because of the unaccustomed passage of the star.
> When the center is shaken, the trembling rocks split in two.
> The veil is torn and the sanctuary lies open to the people.
> Meanwhile, Christ alone, rejoicing, descends into the depths,
> committing his body for burial in the new tomb.[73]

Poetry has a greater power to inspire reflection than a theological treatise. Eriugena's selection of images in the above passage places the reader in the scene—"put before yourself"—and moves the heart toward a response. The two thieves illustrate the opposing manners of seeing Jesus, as well as the radically different outcomes that await man. The signs and portents reveal the great significance of the moment. Most of all, however, Eriugena demonstrates the paradoxical nature of this scene: a "rejoicing" Jesus descends into the depths. The reader should feel moved to choose rightly between the two ways of the thieves and to find hope in the victorious Christ's death.

Humanity's Appropriation of Christ's Passion and Death

Christ's passion and death realize the salvation and redemption of the world not only through a sacrificial exchange and the defeat of Satan, but also by offering an effective example to man. The individual Christian appropriates the model of the incarnate Word's self-immolation upon the cross.

Eriugena develops this *imitatio passionis* through his reading of Maximus the Confessor: "Thus each one who believes in Christ, according to his own virtue and according to the habit and quality of virtue subject to himself, is crucified and crucifies Christ for his own sake, that is, he is 'co-crucified' with Christ."[74] One enters into Christ's passion in order to ascend to divine union.

This co-crucifixion actually takes place through a series of renunciations in which the believer assumes the various degrees of Christ's own

---

73. *Carm.* I, 58–60, 29–38.

74. *Comm.* I, xxxii, 178, 1–4. Jeauneau places the direct citations from Maximus the Confessor in quotation marks. See Maximus, *Ambigua* XLVII, 1360A–1361A.

passion. First, one must be crucified to sin, "taking no part in any of the operations of sin in the flesh and through the flesh."[75] Second, one is crucified to the passions, that is, "to the lower actions of the soul, by which it [the soul] is first corrupted in itself before it acts in the body."[76] Third, there is a dying to "fantasies," that is, "to images of sensible things, which the wise call passions and are formed in the material senses."[77] Fourth, there is the crucifixion to the thoughts and conceptions of the mind, "which draw from sensible things through the corporeal senses."[78] Fifth, "one dies to all sensible things, lest he be seduced through them by error."[79] Sixth, one puts aside "all familiarity and relation that one naturally possesses with sensible things through the flesh."[80] Finally, the believer must "completely extinguish every sensible motion in oneself, as if on a cross."[81] In short, the six crucifixions lead to *theologia*—a pure, transformative, and imageless contemplation of the divine.

Participation in Christ's passion results in an ascent through ever-clearer theophanies, that is, through more and more spiritual understandings of the incarnate Word. Jesus's crucifixion, therefore, realizes and models the believer's return to divine simplicity through separation from the scattered vision of the senses. It reveals the mode of seeing the beauty of creation in God:

> To the degree that each one of the faithful possesses the habit in the mind through increase in virtue, so will he have faith from Christ through an increase in understanding. And as many times that he dies to the modes of his previous and inferior life and is drawn into higher degrees, so his opinions of Christ, although simple, nevertheless will die in him and with him, and he will be borne by intelligence and faith into more sublime theophanies concerning him [the Word]. Thus Christ dies daily in his faithful and is crucified by them, when they destroy the carnal thoughts or the spiritual imperfections that still remain. They ever ascend to

75. *Comm.* I, xxxii, 178, 4–6.

76. *Comm.* I, xxxii, 180, 10–12.

77. *Comm.* I, xxxii, 180, 14–16.

78. *Comm.* I, xxxii, 180, 19–21.

79. *Comm.* I, xxxii, 180, 22–24.

80. *Comm.* I, xxxii, 182, 25–27.

81. *Comm.* I, xxxii, 182, 27–29.

the heights, until they arrive at true knowledge of Christ. The One
Who is Infinite is formed infinitely even in the purest of minds.[82]

The participation in the theophanies of Christ, which give form to
the believer, depends upon the proportion of the separation from vice and
growth in virtue. In order to see who Christ truly is one must struggle to
turn from the deceptions of the world and to assume a new way of life. Asceticism, which encompasses the bodily and spiritual components of man,
offers an imitation of the passion, which is the path of liberation established
by the Lord.[83]

The Descent into Hell

Christ's triumphant harrowing of hell represents a scene of great hope for
the believer. Three poems treat this theme (*Carmina* 6, 7, 9) and portray
Christ's descent as both a victory over Satan and a liberation of righteous
souls. The Son leaves his flesh behind during the three days in the tomb,
bringing light to netherworld and hope to those who awaited their release
for so long:

> After our Salvation had renewed the whole world
> and He had completed all the acts that the Father desired
> exhausted, hanging upon the tree, he rested from the heavy labor.
> In the space of a triple light he destroyed Hades,
> while sleeping under the hard peak of frozen rock
> and fulfilling the prophetic symbols of the prophet-spewing whale.
> Then the pale shadows of souls, from the depths of Hell,
> came forth here and there, marveling at the light that had suddenly arisen
> and was driving away the hideous and fierce specters from the prison.[84]

Jesus's liberation of souls and his dominion over Satan's realm increase
the torments of the wicked and impedes the assaults of evil. Demons, after
the harrowing of hell, can no longer attack the just. "What greater punishment is there for the wicked than to want to act impiously and not be able to
harm anyone? This is the chain with which our Lord Jesus Christ, descend-
ing into Hell, bound the devil. This means that those who believe perfectly

---

82. *Comm.* I, xxxii, 182, 31–44.

83. One cannot follow this way unless he first has faith in Jesus and his passion. Christ
"liberates those who believe in him by virtue of his passion." *Expo.* VIII, ii, 128, 381–82.

84. *Carm.* IX, 90, 1–9.

and piously in Him and keep his commandments cannot be lost."[85] A new state of things begins with Jesus's victory and gift of new hope.

> The great, triumphant light shines forth from Erebus;
> expiring death is stupefied before the beginning of life!

> Now the Word of the Father rules; now virtue, life and salvation
> govern all things; feral death, conquered, is silent.
> The Living One, breaking the bonds of death, has arisen.
> No power is able to restrain God, the most high![86]

Eriugena paints not only a scene of victory, but also a portrait of hope. Christ does not trample upon Satan in an act of perverse vengeance, but rather he transforms hell into a prison for evil forces. The poetry, in particular, moves the faithful toward greater confidence in divine power and life. Those who live in the light of Christ cannot be conquered.[87]

The Resurrection and the Ascension

"Christ has arisen, hence our pious hearts leap with joy; the whole world sings 'Alleluia!' to God."[88] The resurrection of Jesus re-creates the cosmos and reveals the future state of humanity. Jesus rises from the dead as paradisiacal man, freed from the shackles of the carnal body and glorious in his spiritual body; yet he also elevates perfect human nature to a new state, that is, divinized and united with God.

In rising from the dead, on the one hand, Jesus restores the pristine nature of paradise. Man always possessed this state *in potentia*, but, having sinned at the beginning, never actually existed in the truly spiritual manner intended by God. Jesus, in the resurrection, cancels all carnal features of the body and makes man whole again. This healing is manifested in the sexless form of his resurrected body: Jesus appears male to his disciples only in order that they might recognize him: "For he did not rise from the dead in material sex, but as man alone. For in him there is neither male nor female,

---

85. *Peri.* V, 108, 3452–57.

86. *Carm.* VI, 80, 1–2; 21–24.

87. Eriugena adopts a common patristic theme in his poetry. "After Christ, hell is no longer the place where the devil reigns and people suffer but is a prison for the devil himself as well as for those who have voluntarily decided to stay with him and share his fate." Alfeyev, *Conqueror*, 211.

88. *Carm.* V, 77–78, 39–40.

although he did appear in the masculine form—the gender in which he was born from the virgin and in which he suffered—to his disciples after the resurrection in order to confirm their faith in his resurrection."[89]

The post-resurrection appearances of Jesus, though taking place within the limits of time and space, in no way imply that the Lord remains confined to the world of the flesh. His spiritual human body, united perfectly to his divinity, transcends the definitions of the material world.[90] In his earthly appearances, Jesus confirms his disciples' faith, while paradoxically remaining free of fleshly constraints.

In his ascension into heaven, the Word bears his humanity to his rightful place with the Father. The flesh becomes a spiritual body and the spiritual body becomes God. Jesus Christ resolves all divisions in himself and transforms creation through man: "We also read that the celestial powers stand near and minister to God and the Catholic faith testifies that the truly human nature in the Word of God was made God and sits at the right hand of God and reigns."[91] The ascension realizes the final healing and transformation of humanity, the fulfillment of the *admirabile commercium*:

> The Lord, the death of death, rose alive into the heights
> and bore our nature with him to that place.
> Made in the fullness of human nature, he makes that fullness one.[92]

What one now sees in Jesus will belong to all humanity when "all will be one in God." Truly for this reason the Word came: that all might participate in the life of the resurrection and all might be one with God.

Participation in the Resurrection and the Ascension

The Resurrection of Humanity as Given and Gift

Eriugena takes the position that the resurrection of humanity is both innate to human nature and a divine gift that surpasses human nature. On the one hand, the resurrection is natural to human beings. Eriugena cites a

89. *Peri.* II, 19, 383–87.

90. "In no way did he depart from the glory of the resurrection in either place or time or quantity or quality when he manifested himself to his disciples after the resurrection. He held the [same] form in which he appeared to the world, when he was in the world for the sake of the salvation of the world." *Peri.* II, 20, 415–19.

91. *Peri.* II, 66, 1528–31.

92. *Carm.* IX, 90, 29–31.

lengthy passage from Epiphanius, in which the bishop describes examples of natural "resurrections": the passing of day into night, followed by night becoming day; the seed dying in the earth and rising as new plant; hair and finger nails, which appear dead, but grow up again daily; the legends of the resurrected phoenix, doves, and dung-beetles—all of these examples demonstrate a natural capacity for regeneration or rebirth.[93] Eriugena concludes: "If, therefore, there is a natural power at work in the restoration of natural things and in the parts of the human body and in the resuscitation of irrational animals . . . what is surprising if the vital and natural power, which never deserts the substance of human bodies, remains efficacious to the point that, by its operation, bodies themselves are restored to life and to the integrity of the entirety of human nature?"[94] For this reason, the resurrection may be called a "given" of man, since it lies within the definition of the nature itself.

In fact, this innate capacity for resurrection in man extends to all sensibles in creation. As the mediator, man's natural resurrection draws all things with himself in the rising from the dead: "Since all sensible and intelligible things have been created in the plenitude of human nature, is it unreasonable to suggest that the entire world, with all its parts, at the time of the restitution of [human] nature itself, in which the whole is contained, will rise again in a certain kind of general resurrection?"[95] In the end "everything which is naturally created in man necessarily remains whole and uncorrupted."[96] Through man *all* of creation participates in the resurrection to new life.

On the other hand, the resurrection surpasses any natural power. In general, Eriugena voices the principle that "no created substance naturally possesses the power through which it is able to surpass the limits of its nature and immediately, through itself, reach God himself. This is of grace alone and belongs to no natural power."[97] Since the resurrection ultimately entails not only the restoration of the spiritual body, but also divine union, the resurrection requires the grace of Christ for its realization. In the end, "the general resurrection from the dead, of both the good and the bad, will take place in no other way except through the grace of the Redeemer of

93. *Peri.* V, 57–58, 1811–55. Also see Epiphanius, *Ancoratus*, 172C–173C.

94. *Peri.* V, 58, 1856–62.

95. *Peri.* V, 59, 1868–73.

96. *Peri.* IV, 28, 742–44. Also see *Comm.* III, ii, 206, 83–85.

97. *Peri.* II, 68–69, 1574–77.

the world. No natural power could bring this about, to the point that, if the Word-God had not become flesh and lived among men, and had not received the fullness of human nature, in which he suffered and rose, there would be no resurrection from the dead."[98] The grace of Christ is essential not only for the restoration of a natural capacity in man, but it is the *sine qua non* for the resurrection itself: man requires the gift of the incarnate Word for his eternal unity with God.

Eriugena therefore understands the resurrection within the paradoxical relationship between nature and grace. Nature has its own integrity and innate capacities, but those capacities may only be understood within the participation in the divine. The error of fallen man is to see nature only in himself, reduced to pure material immanency apart from God. The resurrection of Christ, however, reveals the essential relationship of man—and all of creation—with the divine: nature may not be understood apart from grace.[99]

The paradox of nature and grace finds its resolution in the mystery of man. All of creation has the natural potential for deification, but cannot realize this potential except through divine gift. Only in man, who contains all things, does one find the effective union of grace and innate capacities that fulfills all of creation. The *Alumnus* summarizes this well:

> You [the *Nutritor*] have given a property to each one [grace and nature]. You have given to nature its coming to be from nothing and its eternal being; to grace you have given the power to deify— that is, to pass into (*transire*) God—those whom the abundance of divine goodness, freely and with neither the support of nature nor previous merits, exalts above all things which are and which are contained within the boundaries of the created universe. But the resurrection of the human substance [person] truly is understood to be common to both these things—I mean, to nature and grace. This is the passing (*transitus*) of mortal bodies into

98. *Peri.* V, 57, 1784–91.

99. After hearing these arguments, the *Alumnus* affirms these conclusions: "For we read that God did no miracle in this world that was contrary to nature. Divine history states that any theophanies of the powers came about through effective and administrated natural powers, when God's command moved them. And if the miracle of miracles is the general resurrection from the dead, the greatest example of which took place first in Christ—for all other natural signs [of the resurrection] may be rightly understood to have taken place as a foreshadowing of His resurrection—would it not be true to say that the resurrection will take place through the effective power of natural causes subject to the divine will?" *Peri.* V, 61, 1948–58.

immortal bodies, of corruptible into incorruptible, from animal into spiritual, from temporal and local into eternal and free of every limitation.[100]

Humanity's Resurrection in Christ

The resurrection begins with the death and dissolution of the body, when the elements are liberated from their carnal state and return to their spiritual state: "The end of man's ruin is the dissolution of the body. The return of nature, therefore, begins with the dissolution of the body. For this reason the death of the flesh is more a useful thing for human nature than a punishment, although it is considered a punishment for sin, to the extent that it is the dissolution of the flesh. This dissolution is generally called death, though it may more reasonably be called the death of death, than the death of flesh."[101] Jesus's own death and resurrection demonstrates this truth: death liberates man and the elements subject to him from the carnal state.

Man will rise, however, as a composite being, since he remains both body and soul. The sacrament of baptism proves this truth, since "men born in Christ through the Holy Spirit are made one with the Spirit itself according to body and soul."[102] Even after the dissolution of the material body, the soul continues to sustain a union with the liberated immaterial elements and, on the day of the resurrection, will reconstitute them as the authentic spiritual body of man:

> Indeed, man does not cease to be man. Man, however, is body and soul. If, however, he is always man, he is therefore always body and soul. And though the parts of man may be separated from one another—for the soul leaves its usual governance of the body it received after generation and, when it leaves, the body dissolves and its parts return to the appropriate places of the elements— nevertheless, by a natural order, the parts do not cease to be related always and inseparably to the whole, and the whole to the parts. Indeed, the order of this relation is never able to perish. Though by corporeal sense they seem to be separated, when we consider this in a deeper sense, we see that it is necessary that they always, at once, and inseparably, subsist together. For the human body,

100. *Peri.* V, 66, 2098–2108.

101. *Peri.* V, 23, 664–69.

102. *Comm.* III, iii, 212, 55–58.

whether it is alive or dead, is the body of a man. In the same way, the human soul, whether it is governing its body in unity, or ceases to rule it, as it appears to the senses, when the body is dissolved into parts, nevertheless it does not cease to be the soul of a man. And thus it is given to understand by a higher understanding of things that the soul rules the body no less when it is in the dispersed elements, than when it was united to it by the complex of its members.[103]

The above passage reveals Eriugena's position regarding the intermediate state of man prior to the general resurrection, as well as his adherence to the truth of the soul-body composite of man. In other passages, he discusses the *anima separata* during its period of waiting for the general resurrection, in which the soul may experience a time of purgation or "sleep" until the resurrection.[104] Yet the soul, in certain sense, remains "embodied" even in this intermediate state through its continuing bond with the dissolved elements of its body: the soul rules the body no less through "the dispersed elements," than it did during the governance it held over the body in this life. Eriugena clearly understands the importance of embodiment in the Christian anthropology. Man must *always* be embodied to be authentically human, even though the one body passes through three different states in its return: 1) the carnal, mortal state of fallen existence; 2) the state of elemental dispersion that remains in a natural relationship with the soul even after death (the intermediate state); and 3) the spiritual state of the resurrection.

In the resurrection, the soul will restore its governance over the immaterial qualities of its body. "For although they [the elements] were superadded to human nature because of sin, nevertheless it is not the case that they do not belong to human nature, since they were added and made by the same Creator of the nature. For this reason, they must be recalled to the unity of nature in the restoration of man, when the soul, at the time of the resurrection, receives the whole that had been subject to it."[105] Thus

---

103. *Peri.* III, 158–59, 4621–38. Also see *Peri.* IV, 86–87, 2538–71.

104. Those who die before the end of the world "await the common resurrection of bodies during the intervening temporal period." *Peri.* V, 167, 5448–53. The soul may experience its purgation "not only during the time of this present life when soul and body spend time together and the body is animated by the soul, but also that temporal space, in which souls, leaving the governance of the body, spend time in another life until they receive their bodies again." *Peri.* IV, 164–65, 5078–83.

105. *Peri.* IV, 86, 2542–47.

man's return to the spiritual state sustains and transforms material creation, reconstituting its authentic immaterial state.

Deification, Divine Union, and Free Participation

The resurrection and deification, though the result of the "given" and the "gift" granted through Christ, do not suppress the contribution of the human will and free choice. We have already seen that, within "being" and "eternal-being," man exercises his creative will in the sphere of "well-being." The application of man's will draws him toward being or non-being, toward authenticity or dissipation. This means that the *manner* of resurrection and eternal-being depends upon the application of human freedom—a human freedom that is called to follow Jesus's path of ascent.

The blessed—those who grew in "well-being" through action and grace—will become God. Deification is "the passage of the saints into God, not only in soul, but also in body, such that they are one in Him and with Him."[106] In becoming God, man is drawn into the Trinitarian life itself: "Thus the Holy Trinity is our θέωσις, that is, deification. For the Trinity deifies our nature, by leading it back through sensible symbols to the height of angelic nature and deifying it in those who pass beyond (*transeunt*) all things into God."[107]

Though Eriugena highlights the Trinitarian nature of deification, he points to Christ as the source of unification and transformation. Christ is, in fact, the primordial deification of man in the eternal divine intention to be incarnate. He is "the greatest and first example of that grace, by which, through no preceding merits, man is rendered God."[108] In Christ, one discovers the summation of God's plan to make creation one with himself.

Christ is not only the eternal exemplar of deification, but he is also the redeemer who restores man's pristine state and elevates him to union with the divine nature: after the Incarnation, one cannot separate the deification through the incarnate Word from salvation through the incarnate Word. Eriugena's poetry reinforces this fundamental theme:

> A wave washes the whole world clean of the old sin;
> blood makes us mortals into gods.[109]

106. *Peri.* V, 217, 7058–61.
107. *Expo.* I, iii, 18, 639–42.
108. *Hom.* XXIII, 310, 10–12.
109. *Carm.* I, 58, 28–29.

> O Christ, Word of God, power, wisdom of the Father,
> a wave of your blood, by which the altar of the cross is bathed,
> cleanses us, redeems us, frees us, and returns life to us,
> and shows to your elect that they are gods.[110]

All deification, therefore, takes place through participation in Christ, who is "every good and giver of all good things. Thus all men may enjoy his fruit by a general participation in natural goods, but the elect alone may enjoy the height of deifications that are in the special return (*specialiter*) beyond every nature."[111] The incarnate Word bestows the gift of salvation and deification upon those who turn towards him and live in him.

Deification, for Eriugena, is not a mechanical process that absorbs all things into the sea of the divine, but rather the integrity of substances will remain even in the intimate unity of divine love. After the return, the repose of all things, "every nature, both corporeal and incorporeal, will be seen to be God alone, with the integrity of nature remaining, such that God, who is incomprehensible through Himself, may be understood in a certain way in the creature, but the creature itself is transformed, by an ineffable miracle, into God."[112] Even the soul-body composite that is man will remain, though preserved in a higher unity: "The property of the natures [body and soul] will remain and their unity will take place; the properties [of each nature] will not take away the unity, nor the unity of the natures the properties."[113] Eriugena likens the union of natures with God to the human voices in a chorus, in which each voice has its integrity and will be perceived in the beauty of the whole song.[114] The various properties of human nature—body, soul, and mind—will be resolved in themselves, and all will be resolved in God, but with no loss of the individual.

As already noted, not all will share the state of deification, although all will be one in God:

> Each one will see by experience what sort of [final] vision he is to receive. For as the Truth says, "In the house of my Father there are many mansions" (John 14:42). There will be phantasies and expressed appearances for each group [the just and the wicked]. The just will have the phantasies of divine contemplations, since God

110. *Carm.* II, 66, 57–60.

111. *Peri.* V, 217, 7043–46.

112. *Peri.* I, 16, 385–89.

113. *Peri.* V, 30, 881–83.

114. See *Peri.* V, 34–35, 1049–64.

will be seen not in Himself, but in certain appearances according to each saint's level of contemplation. . . . But for the impious there will always be the phantasies of mortal things and various false visions according to the different motions of their evil thoughts.[115]

In fact, Eriugena teaches, only the blessed will share in the full grace of deification, while others, who remain at the level of natural goods, will receive one of two states: the enjoyment of the integrity of pristine human nature and all the goods associated with it; or eternal punishment through the fruitless pursuit of self-induced phantasies.[116] This does not mean to say that God's plan has failed: the incarnate Word restores the unity of all things in the divine. Yet it does demonstrate the importance of individual modes of sharing in this unity. While all return to God, this union does not stifle the distinct forms of participation: *who* one is and *how* one is as an individual shapes one's final state of participation in the divine.

Conclusion

The life of Jesus in the Scriptures offers, according to Eriugena, an account of and a program for the return of all things to God. On the one hand, the Scriptures are a historical account of the Word's descent and ascent, from his birth to his return to the Father. Eriugena never overlooks the genuine details of the accounts of Jesus's life in the flesh.

On the other hand, one cannot remain on the level of history, but must pass through the material signs to higher realities. This demands the appropriation of the life of Christ, an imitation of Christ's ascent through action and contemplation. Eriugena summarizes this position regarding the Scriptures in his prayer to Jesus at the conclusion of the *Periphyseon:*

> O Lord Jesus, there is no other prize, no other beatitude, no other joy I could ask of you, but that I may understand your words, which were inspired by the Holy Spirit, in a pure way and free from any error from a false theory. For this is the highest end of my happiness and perfect contemplation, since the rational and even purest mind will find nothing beyond this—because there is nothing beyond this. For just as there is no other place more appropriate to seek you than in your words, so also there is no other place more appropriate to find you than in them. There indeed you

115. *Peri.* V, 119–20, 3839–52.
116. *Peri.* V, 164–65, 5359–68.

live and there you lead those seeking you and loving you. There you prepare a spiritual banquet of true cognition for your elect, and, passing through, you minister to them. And what is your passage (*transitus*), O Lord, except the ascent through the infinite steps of your contemplation? For you always make a passage (*transitus*) in the understandings of those seeking and finding you.[117]

The resurrection and return of humanity, along with all of creation, takes place through Jesus and through an appropriation of his life in contemplation of the Scriptures. The *transitus* from the fallen material body to the life of the spirit, and from the life of the spirit to union with God, demands a full participation in the path of the man-God.

117. *Peri.* V, 210, 6818–6831.

Conclusion

In conclusion, I would like to respond briefly to two questions: What can we learn from the Irishman's teachings on the Incarnation of the Word? What is lacking in his understanding of the Incarnation?

Eriugena's Incarnational Vision

The Centrality of the Incarnation

As noted in the introduction, some scholars critique Eriugena for his failure to appropriate the Fathers'—particularly Maximus the Confessor's—Christocentric vision. One may, they argue, interpret Eriugena's cosmology apart from his teachings on Christ. The Irishman seems to be a traitor to his Christian formation, a philosopher in thrall to a half-understood form of Neoplatonism.

Yet one may apply James McEvoy's words to the case of Eriugena: "The parting of the ways between Platonism and Christianity is the Incarnation of the Word and the doctrine of the mediation of Christ."[1] According to Eriugena, God creates out of love and that love is summarized in the great movement of the divine condescension in the Word-made-flesh. God forms, sustains, and saves creation in the primordial "All-Tree," the incarnate Word, in whom and through whom all things are made, and who is all things. In short, the Incarnation reveals and effects the divine *philanthropia* and desire that "all will be one in God."

Scholars have tended to lose sight of the Incarnation's importance in the blinding light of Eriugena's audacious cosmology. The cosmos' movement from the carnal state, to the condition of spirit, and, finally, to divine union, seems to denigrate material creation as it becomes absorbed into the

1. McEvoy, "Neoplatonism and Christianity," 164.

divine. Yet as we have seen, the Incarnation affects not the destruction of the material world, but a passage *(transitus)* of all things into ever-greater authenticity and divine intimacy. Even matter is not canceled in Jesus's ascension, but rather it is restored to its authentic and glorious spiritual condition in union with the resurrected body. Eriugena understands the Incarnation to effect creation and re-creation and, therefore, he at no time ignores the goodness of the world, even in its fallen state.

A Participatory Christology

Eriugena offers his own form of an *imitatio Christi* through contemplative reading of the Scriptures. His encounter with pseudo-Dionysius and Maximus the Confessor, in particular, gave him a "participatory" understanding of creation, in which the various levels of being depend upon one another and, ultimately, all depend upon God. Creation consists of divinely bestowed givens and gifts, within which man constitutes his manner of existence: man must freely take on the form of Christ.

Eriugena's reading of the historical Jesus in the Scriptures, therefore, seeks to bridge the temporal gap in order that man may enter into the pattern of Christ's ascension. Though this includes the growth in virtue and the separation from vice, the goal of this participation is a sharing in the mystery of the Trinity. Thus all of Eriugena's reflections upon the person of Jesus aim at the highest appropriation of the Christ-form: the intimacy of divine union. The divine-human life of the Word directs man upward, toward the restoration and deification of human nature and, in turn, the elevation of creation through man.

Furthermore, Eriugena includes a sacramental and ecclesial dimension in this imitation of Christ. He teaches that the incarnate Son is the builder of the church, the master of her ministers, and the locus of her graces. Baptism and the Eucharist convey the healing and transforming presence of the Word. Christ continues, therefore, to form believers through his historical presence in the church and in her actions.

A docetic Christology cannot serve as the basis for humanity's participation in God. The enfleshment of God is genuine and essential for the deification of the cosmos. When Eriugena expresses a negative assessment of the flesh and matter, he is lamenting the brokenness of a fallen *state* that must be transformed in Christ, not condemning material creation itself. Thus participation in the ascension of Jesus embraces the material and historical realities as goods in order that they may be raised up to even greater authenticity and glory.

An Environmental Christology

Eriugena's understanding of the Incarnation contributes to the environmental consciousness in two ways. First, it expresses the divine intention to restore *all* of creation. Nothing is excluded from the unification of the created and the uncreated in Christ. God becomes man, not angel, because only man encloses all things in himself and only through man can the effects be transformed. Creation not only expresses a theophany of God— the Creator "creating" himself—but also it possesses the potential of becoming divine through the deep union effected in the Incarnation of the Word.

Second, Eriugena's Christology highlights the responsibility of man toward the created world. Man brought about the great devastation that shrouds creation. The suffering and decay of all living things, the bitter competitions among species, the frustrated desire for transcendence that is evident even in the simplest creature's desire to live—man is the source for these evils that are "without cause." Man, therefore, must also be the instrument of healing, and he can only fulfill that mission through the rebirth in the incarnate Word.

Man's *imitatio Christi*, therefore, elevates all of creation. Following Christ includes not only a greater love for neighbor, but also a sharing in the divine love that calls the cosmos to union. The Word descended, according to Eriugena, to save the effects—his *philanthropia* embraces the world. Each person who follows Christ cannot exclude God's creation from the scope of his or her moral and spiritual life.

Problems in Eriugena's Christology

The Question of Jesus's Two Wills

Eriugena does not overlook the importance of human freedom in the salvation and deification of man. Deification does not take place through an impersonal process, but through the synergy of grace and free human action. In fact, Eriugena's participatory Christology seeks to inspire the free submission to and imitation of the incarnate Word's ascension. Free choice enables man to take on the *forma Christi*.

Unfortunately, Eriugena's understanding of the Incarnation does not offer a sufficient reflection upon the two wills of Christ, divine and human. Maximus the Confessor, who gave his life for this teaching, enriched Christology and Christian anthropology through his profound reflections upon Jesus's exercise of freedom—divine and human—and that freedom's role in the deification of creation.[2] In turn, he contributed greatly to an understanding of personhood and the manner in which man participates in the divine drama of salvation and elevation. Eriugena, lacking this element in his Christology, fails to provide a full anthropological basis for the *personal* human participation in the divine nature.

Does this lacuna cripple Eriugena's development of a "participatory" Christology? Not in the sense that one loses sight of the acting person within the Irishman's understanding of soteriology and deification—he is too good of an Augustinian to allow this to happen. Yet his approach to the *imitatio Christi* would be vastly improved by a treatment of Jesus's two wills: Christ's human nature was deified not only through union with his divine nature, but also through its *free* growth in the divine characteristics of the virtues.[3]

The Problem of Gender Distinctions

Another problem involves Eriugena's rejection of masculine-feminine distinctions in both pre-lapsarian and resurrected humanity. Such differences emerge, according to the Irishman, from the fall as a divinely conceded means for the propagation of the species. After the return, these divisions will be eliminated and humanity will live in God as human alone.

This position becomes evident in his Christology when Eriugena asserts that the resurrected Christ appeared to disciples as "male" in order that they might recognize him. Otherwise, the risen Lord is no longer masculine, but only "human." In order to include all humanity in himself, Jesus can no longer be male.

There are serious problems with this theory. First, it implies that Jesus's gender was purely "docetic"—an appearance or false show for the

---

2. Numerous studies have treated Maximus's understanding of the will. In particular see Gauthier, "La psychologie"; Bathrellos, *The Byzantine Christ*; M. Doucet, "Le monothélisme"; M Doucet, "La Volonté"; Farrrell, *Free Choice*; Lethel, *Agonie*.

3. Perhaps we get a glimpse of this growth when Eriugena states that Christ grew in his humanity through the humble submission to the baptism of John.

sake of his journey in history. This detracts from the authenticity of Word's assumption of flesh. Second, it implies that gender distinctions have no *spiritual* significance, since they are obliterated in the return. Contemporary reflections on male and female spiritualities would certainly challenge such a doctrine. Finally, this theory impedes a genuine *personal* participation in the Christ-form, since persons share in the life of Christ as men and women, not as potentially genderless entities.

Eriugena certainly did not have access to contemporary gender theories and modern personalist philosophies, so it is unjust to fault him too greatly in this regard. Yet nonetheless, his rich understanding of the *imitatio Christi* requires certain corrections to make it relevant for modern concerns. One can rightfully ask: how do men and women personally appropriate the Christ-form according to their masculine-feminine manners of being?

Irish Inspiration

As stated in the introduction, this book purports only to be a modest defense of and introduction to John Scottus Eriugena's understanding of the incarnate Word. Its discussion of the many facets of his thought deserve to be explored and amplified in various directions: his appropriation of the councils in relation to the debates of the period; his spiritual teachings, especially in their Augustinian, Dionysian, and Maximian roots; his influence upon subsequent generations. May the Irishman inspire further reflection upon this great mystery of God's *philanthropia*.

Bibliography

Works of Johannes Scottus Eriugena

Critical Editions

Annotationes in Marcianum. Edited by Cora E. Lutz. Cambridge, MA: Medieval Academy of America, 1939.

Carmina. Edited by Michael W. Herren. SLH 12, 1993. [Latin-Greek text and English translation]

Commentaire sur l'Évangile de Jean [*Commentarius in Sanctum Evangelium secundum Johannem*]. Edited by Édouard A. Jeauneau. SC 180, 1972. [Latin text and French translation]

De divina praedestinatione liber. Edited by Goulven Madec. CCM 50, 1978.

Expositiones in Ierarchiam Coelestem. Edited by J. Barbet. CCM 31, 1975.

Homélie sur le Prologue de Jean [*Homilia in prologum Sancti Evangelii secundum Johannem*]. Edited by Édouard A. Jeauneau. SC 151, 1969. [Latin text and French translation]

Maximi Confessoris Ambigua ad Johannem: iuxta Johannis Scotti Eriugenae latinam interpretationem. Edited by Édouard A. Jeauneau. CCG 18, 1988.

Periphyseon I–V. Edited by Édouard A. Jeauneau. CCM 161–65, 1996, 1997, 1999, 2000, 2003.

Periphyseon I–III. Edited and translated by I. P. Sheldon-Williams. SLH 7, 9, and 11, 1968, 1972, 1981. [Latin text and English translation]

Periphyseon IV. Edited by Édouard A. Jeauneau. Translated by John J. O'Meara and I. P. Sheldon-Williams. SLH 13, 1995. [Latin text and English Translation]

Quaestiones ad Thalassium una cum latina interpretaione Johannis Scotti Eriugenae iuxta posita. Edited by Carl Laga and Carlos Steel. CCG 7 (I–LV) and 22 (LVI–LXV), 1980, 1990. [Greek and Latin Translation]

English Translations

Carmina. Edited by Michael W. Herren. SLH 12, 1993. [Latin-Greek text and English translation]

"Homily of John Scot, the Translator of the *Hierarchy* of Dionysius" [*Homilia in prologum Sancti Evangelii secundum Johannem*]. In John J. O'Meara. *Eriugena*, 158–76. Oxford: Clarendon, 1988.

Periphyseon (The Division of Nature). Translated by I. P. Sheldon-Williams and John J. O'Meara. Montreal: Bellarmin, 1987.

Periphyseon I–III. Edited by I. P. Sheldon-Williams. SLH 7, 9, and 11, 1968, 1972, 1981. [Latin text and English Translation]

Periphyseon IV. Edited by Édouard A. Jeauneau. Translated by John J. O'Meara and I. P. Sheldon-Williams. SLH 13, 1995. [Latin text and English Translation]

Treatise on Divine Predestination. Translated by Mary Brennan. Notre Dame, IN: University of Notre Dame Press, 1998.

The Voice of the Eagle: The Heart of Celtic Christianity [*Homilia in prologum Sancti Evangelii secundum Johannem*]. Translated by Christopher Bamford. Great Barrington, MA: Lindisfarne, 2000.

OTHER ANCIENT WRITERS

Ambrosius Mediolanensis [Ambrose of Milan]. *In Lucam.* Edited by M. Adriaen and P. A. Ballerini. CCL 14, 1957.

Augustinus, Aurelius [Augustine of Hippo]. *De catechizandis rudibus.* Edited by I. B. Bauer. CCL 46, 1969.

———. *De civitate Dei.* Edited by E. Hoffman. CSEL 40, 1877.

———. *De diversis questionibus octoginta tribus.* Edited by Almut Mutzebecher. CCL 44A, 1975.

———. *De Genesi ad litteram.* Edited by J. Zycha. CSEL 28, 1894.

———. *De Genesi contra Manicheos.* Edited Dorthea Weber. CSEL 91, 1998.

———. *In Johannis Evangelium tractatus CXXIV.* Edited by D. Radbodus Willems. CCL 36, 1954. [English translation: *Homilies on the Gospel of John 1–40.* Translated by Edmund Hill. New York: New City, 2009.]

———. *De libero arbitrio.* In *Contra academicos. De beata Vita. De ordine. De magistro. De libero arbitrio,* edited by William M. Green, 204–321. CCL 29, 1970.

———. *De Trinitate libri XV.* Edited by W. J. Mountain. CCL 50, 1968.

Boethius, Ancius Manlius Severinus [Boethius]. *Contra Eutychen et Nestorium.* In *The Theological Tractates and The Consolation of Philosophy,* translated by H. F. Stewart, E. K. Rand, S. J. Tester, 72–129. LCL 74, 1978. [Latin and English translation]

Clemens Alexandrinus [Clement of Alexandria]. *Stromateis VII.* Edited by Alain Le Boulluec. SC 428, 1997. [Greek and French translation]

Dionysius Areopagita [pseudo-Dionysius the Areopagite]. *De caelesti hierarchia.* In *De caelesti hierarchia. De ecclesiastica hierarchia. Theologia mystica,* edited by G. Heil and A.M. Ritter, 7–59. PTS 36, 1981.

———. *De divinis nominibus.* Edited Beate Regina Suchla. PTS 33, 1990.

———. *De ecclesiastica hierarchia.* In *De caelesti hierarchia. De ecclesiastica hierarchia. Theologia mystica,* edited by G. Heil and A. M. Ritter, 61–132. PTS 36, 1981.

———. *Theologia mystica.* In *De caelesti hierarchia. De ecclesiastica hierarchia. Theologia mystica,* edited G. Heil and A. M. Ritter, 139–51. PTS 36, 1981.

Epiphanius [Epiphanius of Salamis]. *Ancoratus.* PG 43, 11–236.

Evagrius Ponticus. *Traité pratique ou le moine* II [*Praktikos*]. Edited by Antoine Guillaumont and Claire Guillaumont. SC 171, 1971. [Greek and French translation]

Gregorius Nazianzenus [Gregory of Nazianzus]. *Orationes XXIX.* In *Discours 27–31,* edited by Paul Gallay, 176–225. SC 250, 1978. [Greek and French translation]

———. *Orationes XL.* In *Discours 38–51,* edited by Claudio Moreschini, 198–311. SC 358, 1990. [Greek and French translation]

Gregorius Nyssenus [Gregory of Nyssa]. *De anima et resurrectione.* PG 46, 11–160.

———. *De beatitudinibus.* In *De oratione dominica. De beatitudinibus,* edited by J. F. Callahan, 75–170. GNO VII/2, 1972.

———. *In Hexaemeron explicatio apologetica.* PG 44, 61–124.

———. *De hominis opificio.* PG 44, 123–256.

———. *Traité de la virginité* [*De virginibus*]. Edited by Michel Aubineau. SC 119, 1966.

Maximus Confessor [Maximus the Confessor]. *Ambigua ad Johannem.* PG 91, 1061–1417.

———. *Capita de caritate.* Edited by A. Ceresa-Gestaldo. Rome: Editrice Studium, 1963. [Greek and Italian translation]

———. *Capita theologica et oeconomica I–II.* PG 90, 1084–1173.

———. *Questiones et dubia.* Edited by J. H. Declerck. CCG 10, 1990.

———. *Quaestiones ad Thalassium una cum latina interpretaione Johannis Scotti Eriugenae iuxta posita.* Edited by Carl Laga and Carlos Steel. CCG 7 (I–LV) and 22 (LVI–LXV), 1980, 1990.

Origenes Alexandrinus [Origen of Alexandria]. *Contre Celse III–IV* [*Contra Celsum III–IV*]. Edited by Marcel Borret. SC 136, 1968. [Latin and French translation]

———. *Homélies sur la Genèse* [*Homiliae in Genesim*]. Edited by W. A. Baehrens. SC 7, 1976. [Latin and French translation]

———. *Traité des principes* [*De principiis*]. Edited by H. Crouzel and M. Simonetti. SC 252 (I–II), 253 (commentary and fragments), 268 (III–IV), and 269 (commentary and fragments), 1978, 1978, 1980, 1980. [Latin and French translation]

Plotinus. *Enneads* [*Enneades*]. Translated by A. H. Armstrong. LCL 440, 445, and 468. 1966, 1966, 1967, 1984, 1984, 1988, 1988. [Greek text and English translation]

Proclus Lycaeus. *Elements of Theology* [*Institutio theologica*]. Translated and edited by E. R. Dodds. Oxford: Oxford University Press, 1963. [Greek and English Translation]

Papers of the Society for the Promotion of Eriugenian Studies (SPES 1973–2002)

The Mind of Eriugena. Papers of a Colloquium. Dublin, 14–18 July 1970. Edited by John J. O'Meara and Ludwig Bieler. Dublin: Irish University Press, 1973.

Jean Scot Érigène et l'histoire de la philosophie. Organisé dans le cadre des colloques internationaux du Centre National de la Recherche Scientifique à Laon, du 7 au 12 juillet 1975. Edited by René Roques. Paris: Éditions du Centre national de la recherche scientifique, 1977.

Eriugena: Studien zu seinen Quellen. Vorträge des III. Internationalen Eriugena-Colloquiums, Freiburg im Breisgau, 27–30. August 1979. Edited by Werner Beierwaltes. Heidelberg: Carl Winter Universitätsverlag, 1980.

Jean Scot écrivain. Actes du IVe colloque international, Montréal, 28 août–2 septembre 1983. Edited by G. H. Allard. Montréal: Bellarmin, 1986.

Eriugena Redivivus. Zur Wirkungsgeschichte seines Denkens im Mittelalter und im Übergang zur Neuzeit. Vorträge des V. Internationalen Eriugena-Colloquiums, Werner-Reimers-Stiftung Bad Homburg, 26–30. August 1985. Edited by Werner Beierwaltes. Heidelberg: Carl Winter Universitätsverlag, 1987.

Giovanni Scoto nel suo Tempo. L'Organizzazione del sapere in età carolingia. Atti del XXIV convegno storico internazionale, Todi, 11–14 ottobre 1987. Edited by C. Leonardi and E. Mesestò. Spoleto: Centro Italiano di Studi sull'Alto Medioevo, 1989.

Begriff und Metapher: Sprachform des Denkens bei Eriugena. Vorträge des VII. Internationalen Eriugena-Colloquiums, Werner-Reimers-Stiftung Bad Homburg, 26–29. Juli 1989. Edited by Werner Beierwaltes. Heidelberg: Carls Winter Universitätsverlag, 1990.

Eriugena: East and West. Papers of the Eighth International Colloquium of the Society for the Promotion of Eriugenian Studies, Chicago and Notre Dame, 18–20 October 1991. Edited by Bernard McGinn and Willemien Otten. Notre Dame: University of Notre Dame Press, 1994.

Johannes Scottus Eriugena: The Bible and Hermeneutics. Proceedings of the Ninth International Colloquium of the Society for the Promotion of Eriugenian Studies, held at Leuven and Louvain-La-Neuve, June 7–10, 1995. Edited by Gerd Van Riel, Carlos Steel and James McEvoy. Leuven: Leuven University Press, 1996.

History and Eschatology in Eriugena and his Age. Proceedings of the Tenth International Conference of the Society for the Promotion of Eriugenian Studies, Maynooth and Dublin, August 16–20, 2000. Edited by Michael Dunne and James McEvoy. Leuven: University Press, 2002.

SECONDARY SOURCES

Alfeyev, Archbishop Hilarion. *Christ the Conqueror of Hell: The Descent into Hades from an Orthodox Perspective.* Crestwood, NY: St. Vladimir's Seminary Press, 2009.

Ansorge, Dirk. *Johannes Scottus Eriugena: Wahrheit als Proceß.* Innsbruck-Wien: Tyrolia-Verlag, 1996.

Arnaldi, Girolamo. "Anastasio Bibliotecario, Carlo il Calvo e la fortuna di Dionigi l'Areopagita nel secolo IX," 513–36. SPES, 1989.

Arnold, Johannes, et al. *Väter der Kirche. Ekklesiales Denken von den Anfängen bis in die Neuzeit.* Paderborn: Schöningh, 2004.

Backus, Irena. *The Reception of the Church Fathers in the West: From the Carolingians to the Maurists.* New York: Brill, 1997.

Bathrellos, Demetrios. *The Byzantine Christ: Person, Nature and Will in the Christology of Saint Maximus the Confessor.* Oxford: Oxford University Press, 2004.

Beeley, Christopher. *The Unity of Christ: Continuity and Conflict in Patristic Tradition.* New Haven: Yale University Press, 2012.

Beierwaltes, Werner. *Eriugena: Grundzüge seines Denkens.* Frankfurt am Main: Vittorio Klostermann, 1994.

———. "Unity and Trinity in East in West," 209–31. SPES, 1984.

Bieler, Ludwig. "Observations on Eriugena's Original Latin Prose," 140–46. SPES, 1973.

Bisogno, Armando. *Il metodo carolingio. Identità culturale e dibattito teolgico nel secolo nono.* Turnhout: Brepols, 2008.

Blowers, Paul. *Drama of the Divine Economy: Creator and Creation in Early Christian Theology and Piety.* Oxford: Oxford University Press, 2012.

———. *Exegesis and Spiritual Pedagogy in Maximus the Confessor: An Investigation of the "Questiones ad Thalassium."* Notre Dame, IN: Notre Dame University Press, 1991.

Blumenthal, Ut-Renate. *Carolingian Essays*. Washington, DC: Catholic University of America Press, 1983.

Böhm, Thomas. "Adnotationes zu Maximus Confessor und Johannes Scottus Eriugena." In *Deutsce Mystik im abendländischen Zusammenhang. Kolloquium Kloster Fischingen 1998*, edited by Walter Haug and Wolfram Schneider-Lastin, 51–60. Tübingen: Miemeyer, 2000.

Brennan, Mary. *Guide des etudes* érigéniennes. *Bibliographie commentée des publications 1930–1987*. Paris: Cerf, 1989.

Cappuyns, Maïeul. *Jean Scot Erigène. Sa vie, son oeuvre, sa pensée*. Bruxelles: Culture et Civilisation, 1964.

Carabine, Deirdre. "Five Wise Virgins: Theosis and Return in *Periphyseon* V," 195–207. SPES, 1996.

———. *John Scottus Eriugena*. New York: Oxford University Press, 2000.

Charles-Edwards, T. M. *Early Christian Ireland*. New York: Cambridge University Press, 2000.

Colish, Marcia. "John the Scot's Christology and Soteriology in Relation to his Greek Sources." *Downside Review* 100 (1982) 138–51.

Coinago, Filippo. *Poesia e teologia in Giovanni Scoto l'Eriugena*. Rome: Herder, 2009.

Contreni, John. "The Irish 'Colony' at Laon During the Time of John Scottus," 59–67. SPES, 1977.

Daley, Brian. *The Hope of the Early Church: A Handbook of Patristic Eschatology*. Peabody, MA: Hendrickson, 2003.

d'Onofrio, Giulio. *Fons scientiae. La dialettica nell'Occidente tardo-antico*. Naples: Liguori, 1986.

———. "The Concordia of Augustine and Dionysius: Toward a Hermeneutic of the Disagreement of Patristic Sources in John the Scot's *Periphyseon*," 115–40. SPES, 1994.

———. *Vera Philosophia. Studies in Late Antique, Early Medieval, and Renaissance Christian Thought*. Translated by John Gavin, S.J. Turnhout: Brepols, 2008.

Doucet, M. "Est-ce le monothélisme a fait autant d'illustres victims?: Réflections sur un ouvrage de F.M. Léthel." *Science et Esprit* 35 (1983) 53–83.

———. "La volonté humaine du Christ, spécialement en son agonie: Maxime le Confesseur, interprète de l'Écriture." *Science et Esprit* 37 (1985) 123–59.

Driscoll, Jeremy. *Steps to Spiritual Perfection: Studies on Spiritual Progress in Evagrius Ponticus*. Mahwah, NJ: Newman, 2005.

Duclow, Donald F. "Divine Nothingness and Self-Creation in John Scotus Eriugena." *Journal of Religion* 57 (1977) 109–23.

———. "Dialectic and Christology in Eriugena's *Periphyseon*." *Dionysius* 4 (1980) 99–117.

Dunne, Michael, and James McEvoy. *The Irish Contribution to European Scholastic Thought*. Dublin: Four Courts, 2009.

Dutton, Paul Edward. "Eriugena, the Royal Poet," 51–80. SPES, 1977.

Erismann, Christophe. "The Logic of Being: Eriugena's Dialectical Ontology." *Vivarium* 45 (2007) 203–18.

Farrell, J. *Free Choice in Maximus the Confessor*. South Canaan, PA: St. Tikhon's Seminary Press, 1989.

Ferguson, Everett. *Baptism in the Early Church: History, Theology, and Liturgy in the First Five Centuries*. Grand Rapids: Eerdmans, 2009.

Finan, Thomas, and Vincent Twomey. *The Relationship between Neoplatonsim and Christianity*. Dublin: Four Courts, 1992.

Foussard, Jean-Claude. "Apparence et apparition: la notion de 'phantasia' chez Jean Scot," 337–48. SPES, 1977.

Gandillac, Maurice de. "Anges et hommes dans le Commentaire de Jean Scot sur la 'Hierarchie Celeste'," 393–403. SPES, 1977.

Ganz, David. "The Debate on Predestination." In *Charles the Bald: Court and Kingdom*, edited by Margaret Gibson and Janet Nelson, 283–302. Oxford: Variorum, 1981.

Garcia, Jorge. "The Ontological Relation Characterization of the Relation between Man and Created Nature in Eriugena." *Journal of History of Philosophy* 16 (1978) 155–66.

Gauthier, R. A. "Saint Maxime le Confesseur et la psychologie de l'acte humain." *Recherches de Théologie Ancienne et Medievale* 21 (1954) 51–100.

Gersh, Stephen. *From Iamblichus to Eriugena: An Investigation of the Prehistory and Evolution of the Pseudo-Dionysian Tradition*. Leiden: Brill, 1978.

———. "Omnipresence in Eriugena: Some Reflections on Augustino-Maximian Elements in the *Periphyseon*," 55–74. SPES, 1980.

Gibson, Margaret, and Janet Nelson. *Charles the Bald: Court and Kingdom*. Oxford: Variorum, 1981.

Hadot, Pierre. *The Veil of Isis: An Essay on the History of the Idea of Nature*. Translated by Michael Chase. Cambridge: Harvard University Press, 2006.

Hankey, Wayne. "Misrepresenting Neoplatonism in Contemporary Christian Dionysian Polemic: Eriugena and Nicholas of Cusa versus Vladimir Lossky and Jean-Luc Marion." *American Catholic Philosophical Quarterly* 82 (2008) 683–703.

———. "The Postmodern Retrieval of Neoplatonism in Jean-Luc Marion and John Milbank and the Origins of Western Subjectivity in Augustine and Eriugena." *Hermathena* 165 (1998) 9–70.

Haug, Walter, and Wolfram Schneider-Lastin. *Deutsce Mystik im abendländischen Zusammenhang. Kolloquium Kloster Fischingen 1998*. Tübingen: Miemeyer, 2000.

Heinzer, Felix, and Christoph Schönborn. *Maximus Confessor: actes du symposium sur Maxime le Confesseur, Fribourg, 2–5 septembre 1980*. Fribourg: Editions Universitaires, 1982.

Jeauneau, Edouard. "La division des sexes chez Grégoire de Nysse et chez Jean Scot Érigíne," 33–54. SPES, 1980.

———. "Jean l'Erigine et les *Ambigua* ad Iohannem de Maxime le Confesseur." In *Maximus Confessor: actes du symposium sur Maxime le Confesseur, Fribourg, 2–5 septembre 1980*, edited by Felix Heinzer and Christoph Schönborn, 343–63. Fribourg: Editions Universitaires, 1982.

———. "The Neoplatonic Themes of *Processio* and *Reditus* in Eriugena." *Dionysius* 15 (1991) 3–29.

———. "Pseudo-Dionysius, Gregory of Nyssa, and Maximus the Confessor in the Works of John Scottus Eriugena." In *Carolingian Essays*, edited by Ut-Renate Blumenthal, 137–49. Washington, DC: Catholic University of America Press, 1983.

Jensen, Robin. *Baptismal Imagery in Early Christianity*. Grand Rapids: Baker Academic, 2012.

Kass, Leon. *The Beginning of Wisdom: Reading Genesis*. Chicago: University of Chicago Press, 2003.

Kavanagh, Catherine. "John Scottus Eriugena and the Uses of Dialectic." In *The Irish Contribution to European Scholastic Thought*, edited by James McEvoy and Michael Dunne, 21–36. Dublin: Four Courts, 2009.

Kijewska, Agnieszka. "The Eriugenian Concept of Theology: John the Evangelist as the Model Theologian," 173–93. SPES, 1996.

Larchet, Jean Claude. *La divinisation de l'homme selon saint Maxime le Confesseur*. Paris: Cerf, 1996.

Léthel, F. M. *Théologie de l'agonie du Christ: la liberté humaine du fils de Dieu et son importance sotériologique mises en lumière par Saint Maxime le Confesseur*. Paris: Beauchesne, 1979.

Lilla, Salvatore. *Dionigi l'Areopagiata e il platonismo cristiano*. Brescia: Morcelliana, 2005.

Lubac, Henri de. *Catholicism: Christ and the Common Destiny of Man*. Translated by Lancelot Sheppard and Elizabeth Englund. San Francisco: Ignatius, 1988.

Luneau, Auguste. *L'histoire du salut chez les pères de l'eglise: la doctrine des ages du monde*. Paris: Beauchesne, 1964.

Madec, Goulven. "Jean Scot et ses auteurs," 143–86. SPES, 1986.

———. "Theologia: note augustino-érigénienne." In *From Augustine to Eriugena: Essays on Neoplatonism and Christianity in Honor of John J. O'Meara*, edited by F. X. Martin and J. A. Richmond, 117–25. Washington, DC: Catholic University Press, 1991.

Marenbon, John. *From the Circle of Alcuin to the School of Auxerre: Logic, Theology and Philosophy in the Early Middle Ages*. Cambridge: Cambridge University Press, 1981.

———. "John Scottus and Carolingian Theology: From the *De Praedestinatione*, Its Background and Its Critics, to the *Periphyseon*." In *Charles the Bald: Court and Kingdom*, edited by Margaret Gibson and Janet Nelson, 303–25. Oxford: Variorum, 1981.

Marler, Jack. "Scriptural Truth in the *Periphyseon*," 155–72. SPES, 1996.

Martin, F. X., and J. A. Richmond, editors. *From Augustine to Eriugena: Essays on Neoplatonism and Christianity in Honor of John J. O'Meara*. Washington, DC: Catholic University Press, 1991.

McCormick, Michael. "Diplomacy and the Carolingian Encounter with Byzantium down to the Accession of Charles the Bald," 15–48. SPES, 1994.

McEvoy, James. "Neoplatonism and Christianity: Influence, Syncretism or Discernment?" In *The Relationship between Neoplatonism and Christianity*, edited by Thomas Finan and Vincent Twomey, 155–70. Dublin: Four Courts, 1992.

———. "'Reditus omnium in superessentialem unitatem': Christ as Universal Saviour in *Periphyseon* V," 366–81. SPES, 1989.

McGinn, Bernard. "Eriugena Mysticus," 235–60. SPES, 1989.

———. "The Originality of Eriugena's Spiritual Exegesis," 55–80. SPES, 1996.

McKitterick, Rosamond. "The Palace School of Charles the Bald." In *Charles the Bald: Court and Kingdom*, edited by Margaret Gibson and Janet Nelson, 384–400. Oxford: Variorum, 1981.

Meyendorff, John. "Remarks on Eastern Patristic Thought in John Scottus Eriugena," 51–67. SPES, 1994.

Mooney, Hilary A. "Der goldene Leuchter. Die ekklesiale Vermittlung der Offenbarung nach Johannes Scottus Eriugena." In *Väter der Kirche. Ekklesiales Denken von den Anfängen bis in die Neuzeit*, edited by Johannes Arnold et al., 563–81. Paderborn: Schöningh, 2004.

————. *Theophany: The Appearing of God according to the Writings of Johannes Scottus Eriugena*. Tübingen: Mohr Siebeck, 2009.

Moran, Dermot. "Idealism in Medieval Philosophy: The Case of Johannes Scottus Eriugena." *Medieval Philosophy and Theology* 8 (1999) 53–82.

————. "Origen and Eriugena: Aspects of Christian Gnosis." In *The Relationship between Neoplatonism and Christianity,* edited by Thomas Finan and Vincent Twomey, 27–53. Dublin: Four Courts, 1992.

————. *The Philosophy of John Scottus Eriugena: A Study of Idealism in the Middle Ages.* New York: Cambridge University Press, 1988.

Nelson, Janet. *Charles the Bald.* New York: Longman, 1992.

————. "The Reign of Charles the Bald: A Survey." In *Charles the Bald: Court and Kingdom,* edited by Margaret Gibson and Janet Nelson, 1–22. Oxford: Variorum, 1981.

O'Meara, Dominic. "The Concept of *Natura* in John Scottus Eriugena (*De divisione naturae Book I*)." *Vivarium* 19 (1981) 126–45.

O'Meara, John J. *Eriugena.* Cork, Ireland: Mercier, 1969.

————. "*Magnorum virorum quondam consensum velimus machinari* (804B): Eriugena's use of Augustine's *De Genesi ad Litteram* in the *Periphyseon,*" 105–16. SPES, 1980.

Oort, Johannes van. "The End is Now: Augustine on History and Eschatology." *HTS Teologiese Studies* 68.1 (2012) 1–7.

Otten, Willemien. *The Anthropology of John Scottus Eriugena.* Leiden: Brill, 1991.

————. "Eriugena's *Periphyseon:* A Carolingian Contribution to the Theological Tradition," 69–93. SPES, 1994.

————. "The Interplay of Nature and Man in the *Periphyseon.*" *Vivarium* 28 (1990) 1–6.

————. "The Pedagogical Aspect of Eriugena's Eschatology: Paradise between the Letter and the Spirit," 509–26. SPES, 2002.

————. "The Role of Man in the Eriugenian Universe: Dependence or Autonomy," 595–609. SPES, 1989.

————. "The Texture of Tradition: The Role of the Church Fathers in Carolingian Theology." In *The Reception of the Church Fathers in the West: From the Carolingians to the Maurists,* edited by Irena Backus, 3–50. New York: Brill, 1997.

Pépin, Jean. "Mysteria et symbola dans le commentaire de Jean Scot sur l'évangile de Saint Jean," 16–30. SPES, 1973.

Perl, Eric. "Metaphysics and Christology in Maximus Confessor and Eriugena," 253–70. SPES, 1994.

————. *Theophany: The Neoplatonic Philosophy of Dionysius the Areopagite.* Albany, NY: State University of New York Press, 2007.

Petroff, Valery. "*Theoriae* of the Return in John Scottus' Eschatology," 527–79. SPES, 2002.

Piemonte, Gustavo. "Image et contenu intelligible dans la conception érigénienne de la 'diffusio dei,'" 80–94. SPES, 1990.

————. "Some Distinctive Theses of Eriugena's Eschatology in his Exegesis of the Gospel according to St. Matthew," 227–42. SPES, 2002.

Radde-Gallwitz, Andrew. *Basil of Caesarea, Gregory of Nyssa, and the Transformation of Divine Simplicity.* Oxford: Oxford University Press, 2009.

Renczes, Philipp Gabriel. *Agir de Dieu et liberté de l'homme: Recherches sur l'anthropologie théologique de saint Maxime le Confesseur.* Paris: Cerf, 2003.

Richardson, Hilary. "Themes in Eriugena's Writings and Early Irish Art," 261–80. SPES, 2002.

Riché, Pierre. "Charles le Chauve et la culture de son temps," 37–46. SPES, 1977.

Riel, Gerd van. "A Bibliographical Survey of Eriugenian Studies 1987–1995," 367–400. SPES, 1996.

———. "Eriugenian Studies 1995–2000," 611–36. SPES, 2002.

Rist, John. *Plotinus: The Road to Reality.* Cambridge: Cambridge University Press, 1967.

Roques, René. *Libres sentiers vers l'érigénisme.* Rome: Edizioni dell'Ateneo Roma, 1975.

Rorem, Paul. *Eriugena's Commentary on the Dionysian Hierarchy.* Toronto: Pontifical Institute for Medieval Studies, 2005.

———. *Pseudo-Dionysius: A Commentary on the Texts and an Introduction to their Influence.* Oxford: Oxford University Press, 1993.

Russell, Norman. *The Doctrine of Deification in the Greek Patristic Tradition.* Oxford: Oxford University Press, 2004.

Schieffer, Rudolf. "Regno e Chiesa sotto Carlo il Calvo," 3–24. SPES, 1989.

Schönborn, Christoph. "Plaisir et douleur dans l'analyse de S. Maxime, d'après les 'Questiones ad Thalassium.'" *Maximus Confessor: actes du symposium sur Maxime le Confesseur, Fribourg, 2–5 septembre 1980,* edited by Felix Heinzer and Christoph Schönborn, 273–84. Fribourg: Editions Universitaires 1982.

Sheldon-Williams, I. P. "Eriugena's Greek Sources," 1–15. SPES, 1973

———. "A List of the Works Doubtfully or Wrongly Attributed to Johannes Scottus Eriugena." *The Journal of Ecclesiastical History* 15.1 (1964) 76–98.

Solignac, Aimé. "La connaissance Angelique." In *La Genese au sens litteral,* edited by A. Solignac and A. Agaesse, 645–53. Paris: Desclée de Brouwer, 1972.

Sorabji, Richard. *Matter, Space and Motion: Theories in Antiquity and their Sequel.* London: Duckworth, 1988.

Steel, Carlos. "The Return of the Body into the Soul: Philosophical Musings on the Resurrection," 581–609. SPES, 2002.

Stephanou, E. "La coexistence initiale du corps et de l'âme d'après saint Grégoire de Nysee et saint Maxime l'Homolgète." *Échos d'Orient* 35 (1932) 304–15.

Stock, Brian. "The Philosophical Anthropology of Johannes Scottus Eriugena." *Studi Medievali* 8 (1967) 1–57.

Studer, Basel. "Zur Soteriologie des Maximus Confessor." In *Maximus Confessor: actes du symposium sur Maxime le Confesseur, Fribourg, 2–5 septembre 1980,* edited by Felix Heinzer and Christoph Schönborn, 239–46. Fribourg: Editions Universitaires, 1982.

TeSelle, Eugene. *Augustine the Theologian.* London: Burns and Oates, 1970.

Thunberg, Lars. *Microcosm and Mediator: The Theological Anthropology of Maximus the Confessor.* Chicago: Open Court, 1995.

Walker, G. S. M. "Erigena's Conception of the Sacraments." *Studies in Church History* III, edited by G. J. Cuming, 150–58. Leiden: Brill, 1966.

Wallis, R. T. *Neoplatonism.* Hackett: Indianapolis, 1972.

Wohlman, Avital. "L'homme et le sensible dans la pensée de Jean Scot Erigène." *Revue Thomiste* 83 (1983) 243–73.

Subject/Name Index

Scripture Index